Magic, Science and Religion

Bronislaw Malinowski

WITH AN INTRODUCTION BY ROBERT REDFIELD

ISBN: 978-1-63923-233-8

Printed: June 2022

Cover Art By: Amit Paul

Published and Distributed By: Lushena Books
607 Country Club Drive, Unit E
Bensenville, IL 60106
www.lushenabooksinc.com/books

ISBN: 978-1-63923-233-8

Magic, Science and Religion

Bronislaw Malinowski

WITH AN INTRODUCTION BY ROBERT REDFIELD

DOUBLEDAY ANCHOR BOOKS

DOUBLEDAY & COMPANY, INC.

GARDEN CITY, NEW YORK

1954

Table of Contents

Introduction

No writer of our times has done more than Bronislaw
Malinowski to bring together in single comprehension the
warm reality of human living and the cool abstractions of
science. His pages have become an almost indispensable
link between the knowing of exotic and remote people as
we know our own neighbors and brothers, and conceptual
and theoretical knowledge about mankind. The novelist of
talent brings particular men and women to our direct acquaintance, but he does not convert this swift and intimate
understanding into the formal generalizations of science.
On the other hand, many scientific students of society state
such general formulations, but without providing that direct acquaintance with real people—that sense of being there
as the work is done or the spell performed—which makes
the abstract generalization truly meaningful and convincing. Malinowski's gift was double: it consisted both in the
genius given usually to artists and in the scientist's power
to see and to declare the universal in the particular. Malinowski's reader is provided with a set of concepts as to religion, magic, science, rite and myth in the course of forming
vivid impressions and understandings of the Trobrianders
into whose life he is so charmingly drawn.

"I shall invite my readers,"—so writes Malinowski—"to step outside the closed study of the theorist into the open air of the Anthropological field . . ." The "Anthropological field" is almost always the Trobriand Islands. Following Malinowski, we are soon "paddling on the lagoon, watching the natives under the blazing sun at their garden work, following them through the patches of jungle; and . . . on the winding beaches and reefs, we shall learn about their life." The life we learn about is both Trobriand life and the life of common humanity. The criticism so often leveled at Malinowski that he generalized from a single case loses much of its force if the assumption may be admitted that there are a common human nature and a universal culture pattern. No writer ever better justified the assumption. We may learn much of all societies from a single society, of all men from a few men, if unusual insight is combined with patient and prolonged study of what other students have written about other societies.

Malinowski looks at the people, then looks back at the books, and then looks again at the people. He does not, as some have done, look at the people, if at all, to find there what the books have told him he should find. The eclecticism of Malinowski's theory is compelled by the fact that the human reality to which he always returns cannot be fully represented by any single theoretical emphasis. Consider how, in the illuminating essay "Magic, Science and Religion" he takes account of the various views of religion which Tylor, Frazer, Marett, and Durkheim have respectively given, and how religion emerges in those pages more multidimensional than in any single account of any one of these other anthropologists. Religion is not only people explaining and projecting their dreams; it is not only a sort of spiritual electric—mana—; it is not solely to be recognized in social communion—no, religion and magic are ways men must have, being men, to make the world acceptable, manageable, and right. And we see the truth of the many-sided view in the windings and twistings of rite and myth, work and worship, in this now well-known island world in New Guinea.

Perhaps it is because he is always so faithful to the reality of the one well-considered, intimately known instance that his method falls short of the requirements of the scientist's formal rule book. If comparisons are made between the Trobriand Islanders and other groups, they are mostly implicit. The materials from the Trobriand Islands, while immensely abundant and rich, are nowhere exposed to us to be fully appraised or to be counted. The notebooks are not opened to us to order and to choose. There is no proof, in any formal sense.

Clyde Kluckhohn[1] has characterized the method as that of "The well-documented anecdote set firmly in a ramified context." This is well said. In the following papers we shall see how often a formulation about society, an insight into human behavior, is established by the vivid recollection of some simple experience in these islands. The description of the natives fishing on the lagoon makes the whole essay on language; the episode about the Trobrianders walking single-file who are interested but not terrorized by hearing a ghost in a yam garden, and several other such stories, make the basis for the discussion of the spirits of the dead and their manifold significance. We are convinced, not by formal proof, but by following Malinowski in his demonstration of the meaning and function of belief and rite in a society, which, while alien to us, we are nevertheless made to feel is ourselves in another form.

Anthropological science, he is in effect telling us, is also an art. It is the art of seeing perceptively a human and social situation. It is the art of taking a warm interest in the particular while seeking in it the universal.

For equally he is telling us that the art of ethnographic insight, fully to perform its task, must become science. In the last pages of the paper on the *Spirits of the Dead* he

[1] Clyde Kluckhohn, "Bronislaw Malinowski, 1884–1942," Jour. Amer. Folklore, Vol. 56, Jul-Sep, 1943, No. 221, pp. 214.

dismisses as false "the cult of 'pure fact'." "There is a form of interpretation of facts without which no scientific observation can possibly be carried on—I mean the interpretation which sees in the endless diversity of facts general laws—which classifies and orders phenomena, and puts them into mutual relationship."

Malinowski's later and more elaborate attempts to order the facts into theoretical systems, notably the two books published after his death, have exposed him to criticism for weakness in the system. But in the papers collected in this volume the theory is simple: it consists chiefly of clarifying distinctions as to some of the principal recurrent and universal kinds of human social behavior, and of stimulating analysis of the ways in which each of these fills the needs of man and maintains the society.

ROBERT REDFIELD

The University of Chicago

Magic, Science and Religion
and Other Essays

Magic, Science and Religion

I. PRIMITIVE MAN AND HIS RELIGION

There are no peoples however primitive without religion
and magic. Nor are there, it must be added at once, any
savage races lacking either in the scientific attitude or in
science, though this lack has been frequently attributed to
them. In every primitive community, studied by trust-
worthy and competent observers, there have been found
two clearly distinguishable domains, the Sacred and the
Profane; in other words, the domain of Magic and Religion
and that of Science.

On the one hand there are the traditional acts and observances, regarded by the natives as sacred, carried out
with reverence and awe, hedged around with prohibitions
and special rules of behavior. Such acts and observances
are always associated with beliefs in supernatural forces,
especially those of magic, or with ideas about beings, spirits,
ghosts, dead ancestors, or gods. On the other hand, a moment's reflection is sufficient to show that no art or craft
however primitive could have been invented or maintained,
no organized form of hunting, fishing, tilling, or search for
food could be carried out without the careful observation

of natural process and a firm belief in its regularity, without the power of reasoning and without confidence in the power of reason; that is, without the rudiments of science.

The credit of having laid the foundations of an anthropological study of religion belongs to Edward B. Tylor. In his well-known theory he maintains that the essence of primitive religion is animism, the belief in spiritual beings, and he shows how this belief has originated in a mistaken but consistent interpretation of dreams, visions, hallucinations, cataleptic states, and similar phenomena. Reflecting on these, the savage philosopher or theologian was led to distinguish the human soul from the body. Now the soul obviously continues to lead an existence after death, for it appears in dreams, haunts the survivors in memories and in visions and apparently influences human destinies. Thus originated the belief in ghosts and the spirits of the dead, in immortality and in a nether world. But man in general, and primitive man in particular, has a tendency to imagine the outer world in his own image. And since animals, plants, and objects move, act, behave, help man or hinder him, they must also be endowed with souls or spirits. Thus animism, the philosophy and the religion of primitive man, has been built up from observations and by inferences, mistaken but comprehensible in a crude and untutored mind.

Tylor's view of primitive religion, important as it was, was based on too narrow a range of facts, and it made early man too contemplative and rational. Recent field work, done by specialists, shows us the savage interested rather in his fishing and gardens, in tribal events and festivities than brooding over dreams and visions, or explaining "doubles" and cataleptic fits, and it reveals also a great many aspects of early religion which cannot be possibly placed in Tylor's scheme of animism.

The extended and deepened outlook of modern anthropology finds its most adequate expression in the learned and inspiring writings of Sir James Frazer. In these he has set forth the three main problems of primitive religion with which present-day anthropology is busy: magic and its relation to religion and science; totemism and the sociological aspect of early faith; the cults of fertility and vegetation. It will be best to discuss these subjects in turn.

Frazer's *Golden Bough*, the great codex of primitive magic, shows clearly that animism is not the only, nor even the dominating belief in primitive culture. Early man seeks above all to control the course of nature for practical ends, and he does it directly, by rite and spell, compelling wind and weather, animals and crops to obey his will. Only much later, finding the limitations of his magical might, does he in fear or hope, in supplication or defiance, appeal to higher beings; that is, to demons, ancestor-spirits or gods. It is in this distinction between direct control on the one hand and propitiation of superior powers on the other that Sir James Frazer sees the difference between religion and magic. Magic, based on man's confidence that he can dominate nature directly, if only he knows the laws which govern it magically, is in this akin to science. Religion, the confession of human impotence in certain matters, lifts man above the magical level, and later on maintains its independence side by side with science, to which magic has to succumb.

This theory of magic and religion has been the starting point of most modern studies of the twin subjects. Professor Preuss in Germany, Dr. Marett in England, and MM. Hubert and Mauss in France have independently set forth certain views, partly in criticism of Frazer, partly following up the lines of his inquiry. These writers point out that similar as they appear, science and magic differ yet radically. Science is born of experience, magic made by tradition. Science is guided by reason and corrected by observation, magic, impervious to both, lives in an atmosphere of mysticism. Science is open to all, a common good of the whole community, magic is occult, taught through mysterious initiations, handed on in a hereditary or at least in very exclusive filiation. While science is based on the conception of natural forces, magic springs from the idea of a certain mystic, impersonal power, which is believed in by most primitive peoples. This power, called *mana* by some Melanesians, *arungquiltha* by certain Australian tribes, *wakan, orenda, manitu* by various American Indians, and nameless elsewhere, is stated to be a well-nigh universal idea found wherever magic flourishes. According to the writers just mentioned we can find among the most primitive peoples and throughout the lower savagery a belief in a supernatural, impersonal force, moving all those agencies which are relevant to the savage and causing all the really important events in the domain of the sacred. Thus *mana*, not animism, is the essence of "pre-animistic religion," and it is also the essence of magic, which is thus radically different from science.

There remains the question, however, what is *mana*, this impersonal force of magic supposed to dominate all forms of early belief? Is it a fundamental idea, an innate category of the primitive mind, or can it be explained by still simpler and more fundamental elements of human psychology or of the reality in which primitive man lives? The most original and important contribution to these problems is given by the late Professor Durkheim, and it touches the other subject, opened up by Sir James Frazer: that of totemism and of the sociological aspect of religion.

Totemism, to quote Frazer's classical definition, "is an intimate relation which is supposed to exist between a group of kindred people on the one side and a species of natural or artificial objects on the other side, which objects are called the totems of the human group." Totemism thus has two sides: it is a mode of social grouping and a religious system of beliefs and practices. As religion, it expresses primitive man's interest in his surroundings, the desire to claim an affinity and to control the most important objects: above all, animal or vegetable species, more rarely useful inanimate objects, very seldom man-made things. As a rule species of animals and plants used for staple food or at any rate edible or useful or ornamental animals are held in a special form of "totemic reverence" and are tabooed to the members of the clan which is associated with the species and which sometimes performs rites and ceremonies for its multiplication. The social aspect of totemism consists in the subdivision of the tribe into minor units, called in anthropology *clans, gentes, sibs,* or *phratries.*

In totemism we see therefore not the result of early man's speculations about mysterious phenomena, but a blend of a utilitarian anxiety about the most necessary objects of his surroundings, with some preoccupation in those which strike his imagination and attract his attention, such as beautiful birds, reptiles and dangerous animals. With our knowledge of what could be called the totemic attitude of mind, primitive religion is seen to be nearer to reality and to the immediate practical life interests of the savage, than it appeared in its "animistic" aspect emphasized by Tylor and the earlier anthropologists.

By its apparently strange association with a problematic form of social division, I mean the clan system; totemism has taught anthropology yet another lesson: it has revealed the importance of the sociological aspect in all the early forms of cult. The savage depends upon the group with whom he is in direct contact both for practical co-operation and mental solidarity to a far larger extent than does civilized man. Since—as can be seen in totemism, magic, and many other practices—early cult and ritual are closely associated with practical concerns as well as with mental needs, there must exist an intimate connection between social organization and religious belief. This was understood already by that pioneer of religious anthropology, Robertson Smith, whose principle that primitive religion "was essentially an affair of the community rather than of individuals" has become a *Leitmotiv* of modern research. According to Professor Durkheim, who has put these views most forcibly, "the religious" is identical with "the social." For "in a general way . . . a society has all that is necessary to arouse the sensation of the Divine in minds, merely by the power that it has over them; for to its members it is what a God is to its worshippers."[1] Professor Durkheim

[1] *The Elementary Forms of the Religious Life,* p. 206.

arrives at this conclusion by the study of totemism, which
he believes to be the most primitive form of religion. In
this the "totemic principle" which is identical with *mana*
and with "the God of the clan . . . can be nothing else
than the clan itself." [2]

These strange and somewhat obscure conclusions will be
criticized later, and it will be shown in what consists the
grain of truth they undoubtedly contain and how fruitful
it can be. It has borne fruit, in fact, in influencing some of
the most important writing of mixed classical scholarship
and anthropology, to mention only the works of Miss Jane
Harrison and Mr. Cornford.

The third great subject introduced into the Science of
Religion by Sir James Frazer is that of the cults of vegetation and fertility. In *The Golden Bough*, starting from the
awful and mysterious ritual of the wood divinities at Nemi,
we are led through an amazing variety of magical and religious cults, devised by man to stimulate and control the
fertilizing work of skies and earth and of sun and rain,
and we are left with the impression that early religion is
teeming with the forces of savage life, with its young beauty
and crudity, with its exuberance and strength so violent
that it leads now and again to suicidal acts of self-immola-
tion. The study of *The Golden Bough* shows us that for
primitive man death has meaning mainly as a step to
resurrection, decay as a stage of rebirth, the plenty of au-
tumn and the decline of winter as preludes to the revival
of spring. Inspired by these passages of *The Golden Bough*
a number of writers have developed, often with greater
precision and with a fuller analysis than by Frazer himself,
what could be called the *vitalistic* view of religion. Thus
Mr. Crawley in his *Tree of Life*, M. van Gennep in his
Rites de Passage, and Miss Jane Harrison in several works,
have given evidence that faith and cult spring from the
crises of human existence, "the great events of life, birth,
adolescence, marriage, death . . . it is about these events

[2] *Ibid.*

that religion largely focuses."[8] The tension of instinctive need, strong emotional experiences, lead in some way or other to cult and belief. "Art and Religion alike spring from unsatisfied desire."[4] How much truth there is in this somewhat vague statement and how much exaggeration we shall be able to assess later on.

There are two important contributions to the theory of primitive religion which I mention here only, for they have somehow remained outside the main current of anthropological interest. They treat of the primitive idea of one God and of the place of morals in primitive religion respectively. It is remarkable that they have been and still are neglected, for are not these two questions first and foremost in the mind of anyone who studies religion, however crude and rudimentary it may be? Perhaps the explanation is in the preconceived idea that "origins" must be very crude and simple and different from the "developed forms," or else in the notion that the "savage" or "primitive" is really savage and primitive!

The late Andrew Lang indicated the existence among some Australian natives of the belief in a tribal All-Father, and the Rev. Pater Wilhelm Schmidt has adduced much evidence proving that this belief is universal among all the peoples of the simplest cultures and that it cannot be discarded as an irrelevant fragment of mythology, still less as an echo of missionary teaching. It looks, according to Pater Schmidt, very much like an indication of a simple and pure form of early monotheism.

The problem of morals as an early religious function was also left on one side, until it received an exhaustive treatment, not only in the writings of Pater Schmidt but also and notably in two works of outstanding importance: the *Origin and Development of Moral Ideas* of Professor E. Westermarck, and *Morals in Evolution* of Professor L. T. Hobhouse.

[8] J. Harrison, *Themis*, p. 42.

[4] J. Harrison, op. cit. p. 44.

It is not easy to summarize concisely the trend of anthropological studies in our subject. On the whole it has been towards an increasingly elastic and comprehensive view of religion. Tylor had still to refute the fallacy that there are primitive peoples without religion. Today we are somewhat perplexed by the discovery that to a savage· all is religion, that he perpetually lives in a world of mysticism and ritualism. If religion is co-extensive with "life" and with "death" into the bargain, if it arises from all "collective" acts and from all "crises in the individual's existence," if it comprises all savage "theory" and covers all his "practical concerns"—we are led to ask, not without dismay: What remains outside it, what is the world of the "profane" in primitive life? Here is a first problem into which modern anthropology, by the number of contradictory views, has thrown some confusion, as can be seen even from the above short sketch. We shall be able to contribute towards its solution in the next section.

Primitive religion, as fashioned by modern anthropology, has been made to harbor all sorts of heterogeneous things. At first reserved in animism for the solemn figures of ancestral spirits, ghosts and souls, besides a few fetishes, it had gradually to admit the thin, fluid, ubiquitous *mana*; then, like Noah's Ark, it was with the introduction of totemism loaded with beasts, not in pairs but in shoals and species, joined by plants, objects, and even manufactured articles; then came human activities and concerns and the gigantic ghost of the Collective Soul, Society Divinized. Can there be any order or system put into this medley of apparently unrelated objects and principles? This question will occupy us in the third section.

One achievement of modern anthropology we shall not question: the recognition that magic and religion are not merely a doctrine or a philosophy, not merely an intellectual body of opinion, but a special mode of behavior, a pragmatic attitude built up of reason, feeling, and will alike. It is a mode of action as well as a system of belief, and a sociological phenomenon as well as a personal experience. But with all this, the exact relation between the social and the individual contributions to religion is not clear, as we have seen from the exaggerations committed on either side. Nor is it clear what are the respective shares of emotion and reason. All these questions will have to be dealt with by future anthropology, and it will be possible only to suggest solutions and indicate lines of argument in this short essay.

II. RATIONAL MASTERY BY MAN OF HIS SURROUNDINGS

The problem of primitive knowledge has been singularly neglected by anthropology. Studies on savage psychology were exclusively confined to early religion, magic and mythology. Only recently the work of several English, German, and French writers, notably the daring and brilliant speculations of Professor Lévy-Bruhl, gave an impetus to the student's interest in what the savage does in his more sober moods. The results were startling indeed: Professor Lévy-Bruhl tells us, to put it in a nutshell, that primitive man has no sober moods at all, that he is hopelessly and completely immersed in a mystical frame of mind. Incapable of dispassionate and consistent observation, devoid of the power of abstraction, hampered by "a decided aversion towards reasoning," he is unable to draw any benefit from experience, to construct or comprehend even the most elementary laws of nature. "For minds thus orientated there is no fact purely physical." Nor can there exist for them any clear idea of substance and attribute, cause and effect, identity and contradiction. Their outlook is that of confused superstition, "prelogical," made of mystic "participations" and "exclusions." I have here summarized a body of opinion, of which the brilliant French sociologist is the most decided and competent spokesman, but which numbers besides, many anthropologists and philosophers of renown.

But there are also dissenting voices. When a scholar and

anthropologist of the measure of Professor J. L. Myres en-
titles an article in *Notes and Queries* "Natural Science,"
and when we read there that the savage's "knowledge based
on observation is distinct and accurate," we must surely
pause before accepting primitive man's irrationality as a
dogma. Another highly competent writer, Dr. A. A. Golden-
weiser, speaking about primitive "discoveries, inventions
and improvements"—which could hardly be attributed to
any pre-empirical or prelogical mind—affirms that "it
would be unwise to ascribe to the primitive mechanic
merely a passive part in the origination of inventions. Many
a happy thought must have crossed his mind, nor was he
wholly unfamiliar with the thrill that comes from an idea
effective in action." Here we see the savage endowed with
an attitude of mind wholly akin to that of a modern man
of science!

To bridge over the wide gap between the two extreme
opinions current on the subject of primitive man's reason,
it will be best to resolve the problem into two questions.

First, has the savage any rational outlook, any rational
mastery of his surroundings, or is he, as M. Lévy-Bruhl and
his school maintain, entirely "mystical"? The answer will
be that every primitive community is in possession of a
considerable store of knowledge, based on experience and
fashioned by reason.

The second question then opens: Can this primitive
knowledge be regarded as a rudimentary form of science or
is it, on the contrary, radically different, a crude empiry, a
body of practical and technical abilities, rules of thumb
and rules of art having no theoretical value? This second
question, epistemological rather than belonging to the
study of man, will be barely touched upon at the end of this
section and a tentative answer only will be given.

In dealing with the first question, we shall have to ex-
amine the "profane" side of life, the arts, crafts and
economic pursuits, and we shall attempt to disentangle in
it a type of behavior, clearly marked off from magic and
religion, based on empirical knowledge and on the con-

fidence in logic. We shall try to find whether the lines of such behavior are defined by traditional rules, known, perhaps even discussed sometimes, and tested. We shall have to inquire whether the sociological setting of the rational and empirical behavior differs from that of ritual and cult. Above all we shall ask, do the natives distinguish the two domains and keep them apart, or is the field of knowledge constantly swamped by superstition, ritualism, magic or religion?

Since in the matter under discussion there is an appalling lack of relevant and reliable observations, I shall have largely to draw upon my own material, mostly unpublished, collected during a few years' field work among the Melanesian and Papuo-Melanesian tribes of Eastern New Guinea and the surrounding archipelagoes. As the Melanesians are reputed, however, to be specially magic-ridden, they will furnish an acid test of the existence of empirical and rational knowledge among savages living in the age of polished stone.

These natives, and I am speaking mainly of the Melanesians who inhabit the coral atolls to the N.E. of the main island, the Trobriand Archipelago and the adjoining groups, are expert fishermen, industrious manufacturers and traders, but they rely mainly on gardening for their subsistence. With the most rudimentary implements, a pointed digging-stick and a small axe, they are able to raise crops sufficient to maintain a dense population and even yielding a surplus, which in olden days was allowed to rot unconsumed, and which at present is exported to feed plantation hands. The success in their agriculture depends—besides the excellent natural conditions with which they are favored—upon their extensive knowledge of the classes of the soil, of the various cultivated plants, of the mutual adaptation of these two factors, and, last not least, upon their knowledge of the importance of accurate and hard work. They have to select the soil and the seedlings, they have appropriately to fix the times for clearing and burning the scrub, for planting and weeding, for training the vines of the yam plants. In all this they are guided by a clear knowledge of weather and seasons, plants and pests, soil and tubers, and by a conviction that this knowledge is true and reliable, that it can be counted upon and must be scrupulously obeyed.

Yet mixed with all their activities there is to be found magic, a series of rites performed every year over the gardens in rigorous sequence and order. Since the leadership in garden work is in the hands of the magician, and since ritual and practical work are intimately associated, a superficial observer might be led to assume that the mystic and the rational behavior are mixed up, that their effects are not distinguished by the natives and not distinguishable in scientific analysis. Is this so really?

Magic is undoubtedly regarded by the natives as absolutely indispensable to the welfare of the gardens. What would happen without it no one can exactly tell, for no native garden has ever been made without its ritual, in spite of some thirty years of European rule and missionary influence and well over a century's contact with white traders. But certainly various kinds of disaster, blight, unseasonable droughts rains, bush-pigs and locusts, would destroy the unhallowed garden made without magic.

Does this mean, however, that the natives attribute all the good results to magic? Certainly not. If you were to suggest to a native that he should make his garden mainly by magic and scamp his work, he would simply smile on your simplicity. He knows as well as you do that there are natural conditions and causes, and by his observations he knows also that he is able to control these natural forces by mental and physical effort. His knowledge is limited, no doubt, but as far as it goes it is sound and proof against mysticism. If the fences are broken down, if the seed is destroyed or has been dried or washed away, he will have recourse not to magic, but to work, guided by knowledge and reason. His experience has taught him also, on the other hand, that in spite of all his forethought and beyond all his efforts there are agencies and forces which one year bestow unwonted and unearned benefits of fertility, making everything run smooth and well, rain and sun appear at the right moment, noxious insects remain in abeyance, the harvest yields a superabundant crop; and another year again the same agencies bring ill luck and bad chance, pursue him from beginning till end and thwart all his most strenuous efforts and his best-founded knowledge. To control these influences and these only he employs magic.

Thus there is a clear-cut division: there is first the well-known set of conditions, the natural course of growth, as well as the ordinary pests and dangers to be warded off by fencing and weeding. On the other hand there is the domain of the unaccountable and adverse influences, as well as the great unearned increment of fortunate coincidence. The first conditions are coped with by knowledge and work, the second by magic.

This line of division can also be traced in the social setting of work and ritual respectively. Though the garden magician is, as a rule, also the leader in practical activities, these two functions are kept strictly apart. Every magical ceremony has its distinctive name, its appropriate time and its place in the scheme of work, and it stands out of the ordinary course of activities completely. Some of them are ceremonial and have to be attended by the whole community, all are public in that it is known when they are going to happen and anyone can attend them. They are performed on selected plots within the gardens and on a special corner of this plot. Work is always tabooed on such occasions, sometimes only while the ceremony lasts, sometimes for a day or two. In his lay character the leader and magician directs the work, fixes the dates for starting, harangues and exhorts slack or careless gardeners. But the two roles never overlap or interfere: they are always clear, and any native will inform you without hesitation whether the man acts as magician or as leader in garden work.

What has been said about gardens can be paralleled from any one of the many other activities in which work and magic run side by side without ever mixing. Thus in canoe building empirical knowledge of material, of technology, and of certain principles of stability and hydrodynamics, function in company and close association with magic, each yet uncontaminated by the other.

For example, they understand perfectly well that the wider the span of the outrigger the greater the stability yet the smaller the resistance against strain. They can clearly explain why they have to give this span a certain traditional width, measured in fractions of the length of the dugout. They can also explain, in rudimentary but clearly mechanical terms, how they have to behave in a sudden gale, why the outrigger must be always on the weather side, why the one type of canoe can and the other cannot beat. They have, in fact, a whole system of principles of sailing, embodied in a complex and rich terminology, traditionally handed on and obeyed as rationally and consistently as is modern science by modern sailors. How could they sail otherwise under eminently dangerous conditions in their frail primitive craft?

But even with all their systematic knowledge, methodically applied, they are still at the mercy of powerful and incalculable tides, sudden gales during the monsoon season and unknown reefs. And here comes in their magic, performed over the canoe during its construction, carried out at the beginning and in the course of expeditions and resorted to in moments of real danger. If the modern seaman, entrenched in science and reason, provided with all sorts of safety appliances, sailing on steel-built steamers, if even he has a singular tendency to superstition—which does not rob him of his knowledge or reason, nor make him altogether prelogical—can we wonder that his savage colleague, under much more precarious conditions, holds fast to the safety and comfort of magic?

An interesting and crucial test is provided by fishing in the Trobriand Islands and its magic. While in the villages on the inner lagoon fishing is done in an easy and absolutely reliable manner by the method of poisoning, yielding abundant results without danger and uncertainty, there are on the shores of the open sea dangerous modes of fishing and also certain types in which the yield greatly varies according to whether shoals of fish appear beforehand or not. It is most significant that in the lagoon fishing, where man can rely completely upon his knowledge and skill, magic does not exist, while in the open-sea fishing, full of danger and uncertainty, there is extensive magical ritual to secure safety and good results.

Again, in warfare the natives know that strength, courage, and agility play a decisive part. Yet here also they practice magic to master the elements of chance and luck.

Nowhere is the duality of natural and supernatural causes divided by a line so thin and intricate, yet, if carefully followed up, so well marked, decisive, and instructive, as in the two most fateful forces of human destiny: health and death. Health to the Melanesians is a natural state of affairs and, unless tampered with, the human body will remain in perfect order. But the natives know perfectly well that there are natural means which can affect health and even destroy the body. Poisons, wounds, burns, falls, are known to cause disablement or death in a natural way. And this is not a matter of private opinion of this or that individual, but it is laid down in traditional lore and even in belief, for there are considered to be different ways to the nether world for those who died by sorcery and those who met "natural" death. Again, it is recognized that cold, heat, overstrain, too much sun, overeating, can all cause minor ailments, which are treated by natural remedies such as massage, steaming, warming at a fire and certain potions. Old age is known to lead to bodily decay and the explanation is given by the natives that very old people grow weak, their oesophagus closes up, and therefore they must die.

But besides these natural causes there is the enormous domain of sorcery and by far the most cases of illness and death are ascribed to this. The line of distinction between sorcery and the other causes is clear in theory and in most cases of practice, but it must be realized that it is subject to what could be called the personal perspective. That is, the more closely a case has to do with the person who considers it, the less will it be "natural," the more "magical." Thus a very old man, whose pending death will be considered natural by the other members of the community, will be afraid only of sorcery and never think of his natural fate. A fairly sick person will diagnose sorcery in his own case, while all the others might speak of too much betel nut or overeating or some other indulgence.

But who of us really believes that his own bodily infirmities and the approaching death is a purely natural occurrence, just an insignificant event in the infinite chain of causes? To the most rational of civilized men health, disease, the threat of death, float in a hazy emotional mist, which seems to become denser and more impenetrable as the fateful forms approach. It is indeed astonishing that "savages" can achieve such a sober, dispassionate outlook in these matters as they actually do.

Thus in his relation to nature and destiny, whether he tries to exploit the first or to dodge the second, primitive man recognizes both the natural and the supernatural forces and agencies, and he tries to use them both for his benefit. Whenever he has been taught by experience that effort guided by knowledge is of some avail, he never spares the one or ignores the other. He knows that a plant cannot grow by magic alone, or a canoe sail or float without being properly constructed and managed, or a fight be won without skill and daring. He never relies on magic alone, while, on the contrary, he sometimes dispenses with it completely, as in fire-making and in a number of crafts and pursuits. But he clings to it, whenever he has to recognize the impotence of his knowledge and of his rational technique.

I have given my reasons why in this argument I had to rely principally on the material collected in the classical land of magic, Melanesia. But the facts discussed are so fundamental, the conclusions drawn of such a general nature, that it will be easy to check them on any modern detailed ethnographic record. Comparing agricultural work and magic, the building of canoes, the art of healing by magic and by natural remedies, the ideas about the causes of death in other regions, the universal validity of what has been established here could easily be proved. Only, since no observations have methodically been made with reference to the problem of primitive knowledge, the data from other writers could be gleaned only piecemeal and their testimony though clear would be indirect.

I have chosen to face the question of primitive man's rational knowledge directly: watching him at his principal occupations, seeing him pass from work to magic and back again, entering into his mind, listening to his opinions. The whole problem might have been approached through the avenue of language, but this would have led us too far into questions of logic, semasiology, and theory of primitive languages. Words which serve to express general ideas such as *existence, substance,* and *attribute, cause* and *effect,* the *fundamental* and the *secondary;* words and expressions used in complicated pursuits like sailing, construction, measuring and checking; numerals and quantitative descriptions, correct and detailed classifications of natural phenomena, plants and animals—all this would lead us exactly to the same conclusion: that primitive man can observe and think, and that he possesses, embodied in his language, systems of methodical though rudimentary knowledge.

Similar conclusions could be drawn from an examination of those mental schemes and physical contrivances which could be described as diagrams or formulas. Methods of indicating the main points of the compass, arrangements of stars into constellations, co-ordination of these with the seasons, naming of moons in the year, of quarters in the moon—all these accomplishments are known to the simplest savages. Also they are all able to draw diagrammatic maps in the sand or dust, indicate arrangements by placing small stones, shells, or sticks on the ground, plan expeditions or raids on such rudimentary charts. By co-ordinating space and time they are able to arrange big tribal gatherings and to combine vast tribal movements over extensive areas.[1] The use of leaves, notched sticks, and similar aids to memory is well known and seems to be almost universal. All such "diagrams" are means of reducing a complex and unwieldy bit of reality to a simple and handy form. They give man a relatively easy mental control over it. As such are they not—in a very rudimentary form no doubt—fundamentally akin to developed scientific formulas and "models," which are also simple and handy paraphrases of a complex or abstract reality, giving the civilized physicist mental control over it?

This brings us to the second question: Can we regard primitive knowledge, which, as we found, is both empirical and rational, as a rudimentary stage of science, or is it not at all related to it? If by science be understood a body of rules and conceptions, based on experience and derived from it by logical inference, embodied in material achievements and in a fixed form of tradition and carried on by some sort of social organization—then there is no doubt that even the lowest savage communities have the beginnings of science, however rudimentary.

Most epistemologists would not, however, be satisfied with such a "minimum definition" of science, for it might apply to the rules of an art or craft as well. They would maintain that the rules of science must be laid down explicitly, open to control by experiment and critique by reason. They must not only be rules of practical behavior, but theoretical laws of knowledge. Even accepting this stricture, however, there is hardly any doubt that many of the principles of savage knowledge are scientific in this sense. The native shipwright knows not only practically of buoyancy, leverage, equilibrium, he has to obey these laws not only on water, but while making the canoe he must have the principles in his mind. He instructs his helpers in them. He gives them the traditional rules, and in a crude and simple manner, using his hands, pieces of wood, and a limited technical vocabulary, he explains some general laws

[1] Cf. the writer's *Argonauts of the Western Pacific*, chap. xvi.

of hydrodynamics and equilibrium. Science is not detached from the craft, that is certainly true, it is only a means to an end, it is crude, rudimentary, and inchoate, but with all that it is the matrix from which the higher developments must have sprung.

If we applied another criterion yet, that of the really scientific attitude, the disinterested search for knowledge and for the understanding of causes and reasons, the answer would certainly not be in a direct negative. There is, of course, no widespread thirst for knowledge in a savage community, new things such as European topics bore them frankly and their whole interest is largely encompassed by the traditional world of their culture. But within this there is both the antiquarian mind passionately interested in myths, stories, details of customs, pedigrees, and ancient happenings, and there is also to be found the naturalist, patient and painstaking in his observations, capable of generalization and of connecting long chains of events in the life of animals, and in the marine world or in the jungle. It is enough to realize how much European naturalists have often learned from their savage colleagues to appreciate this interest found in the native for nature. There is finally among the primitives, as every fieldworker well knows, the sociologist, the ideal informant, capable with marvelous accuracy and insight to give the *raison d'être*, the function, and the organization of many a simpler institution in his tribe.

Science, of course, does not exist in any uncivilized community as a driving power, criticizing, renewing, constructing. Science is never consciously made. But on this criterion, neither is there law, nor religion, nor government among savages.

The question, however, whether we should call it *science* or only *empirical and rational knowledge* is not of primary importance in this context. We have tried to gain a clear idea as to whether the savage has only one domain of reality or two, and we found that he has his profane world of practical activities and rational outlook besides the sacred region of cult and belief. We have been able to map out the two domains and to give a more detailed description of the one. We must now pass to the second.

III. LIFE, DEATH, AND DESTINY IN EARLY FAITH AND CULT

We pass now to the domain of the *sacred*, to religious and magical creeds and rites. Our historical survey of theories has left us somewhat bewildered with the chaos of opinions and with the jumble of phenomena. While it was difficult not to admit into the enclosure of religion one after the other, spirits and ghosts, totems and social events, death and life, yet in the process religion seemed to become a thing more and more confused, both an all and a nothing. It certainly cannot be defined by its subject matter in a narrow sense, as "spirit worship," or as "ancestor cult," or as the "cult of nature." It includes animism, animatism, totemism, and fetishism, but it is not any one of them exclusively. The *ism* definition of religion in its origins must be given up, for religion does not cling to any one object or class of objects, though incidentally it can touch and hallow all. Nor, as we have seen, is religion identical with Society or the Social, nor can we remain satisfied by a vague hint that it clings to life only, for death opens perhaps the vastest view on to the other world. As an "appeal to higher powers," religion can only be distinguished from magic and not defined in general, but even this view will have to be slightly modified and supplemented.

The problem before us is, then, to try to put some order into the facts. This will allow us to determine somewhat more precisely the character of the domain of the *Sacred* and mark it off from that of the *Profane*. It will also give us an opportunity to state the relation between magic and religion.

1. THE CREATIVE ACTS OF RELIGION It will be best to face the facts first and, in order not to narrow down the scope of the survey, to take as our watchword the vaguest and most general of indices: "Life." As a matter of fact, even a slight acquaintance with ethnological literature is enough to convince anyone that in reality the physiological phases of human life, and, above all, its crises, such as conception, pregnancy, birth, puberty, marriage, and death, form the nuclei of numerous rites and beliefs. Thus beliefs about conception, such as that in reincarnation, spirit-entry, magical impregnation, exist in one form or another in almost every tribe, and they are often associated with rites and observances. During pregnancy the expectant mother has to keep certain taboos and undergo ceremonies, and her husband shares at times in both. At birth, before and after, there are various magical rites to prevent dangers and undo sorcery, ceremonies of purification, communal rejoicings and acts of presentation of the newborn to higher powers or to the community. Later on in life the boys and, much less frequently, the girls have to undergo the often protracted rites of initiation, as a rule shrouded in mystery and marred by cruel and obscene ordeals.

Without going any further, we can see that even the very beginnings of human life are surrounded by an inextricably mixed-up medley of beliefs and rites. They seem to be strongly attracted by any important event in life, to crystallize around it, surround it with a rigid crust of formalism and ritualism—but to what purpose? Since we cannot define cult and creed by their objects, perhaps it will be possible to perceive their function.

A closer scrutiny of the facts allows us to make from the outset a preliminary classification into two main groups. Compare a rite carried out to prevent death in childbed with another typical custom, a ceremony in celebration of a birth. The first rite is carried out as a means to an end, it has a definite practical purpose which is known to all who

practice it and can be easily elicited from any native informant. The post-natal ceremony, say a presentation of a newborn or a feast of rejoicing in the event, has no purpose:
it is not a means to an end but an end in itself. It expresses
the feelings of the mother, the father, the relatives, the
whole community, but there is no future event which this
ceremony foreshadows, which it is meant to bring about or
to prevent. This difference will serve us as a *prima facie*
distinction between magic and religion. While in the magical act the underlying idea and aim is always clear, straightforward, and definite, in the religious ceremony there is no
purpose directed toward a subsequent event. It is only possible for the sociologist to establish the function, the sociological *raison d'être* of the act. The native can always state
the end of the magical rite, but he will say of a religious
ceremony that it is done because such is the usage, or because it has been ordained, or he will narrate an explanatory
myth.

In order to grasp better the nature of primitive religious
ceremonies and their function, let us analyze the ceremonies
of initiation. They present right through the vast range of
their occurrence certain striking similarities. Thus the novices have to undergo a more or less protracted period of
seclusion and preparation. Then comes initiation proper,
in which the youth, passing through a series of ordeals, is
finally submitted to an act of bodily mutilation: at the
mildest, a slight incision or the knocking out of a tooth;
or, more severe, circumcision; or, really cruel and dangerous, an operation such as the subincision practiced in some
Australian tribes. The ordeal is usually associated with the
idea of the death and rebirth of the initiated one, which is
sometimes enacted in a mimetic performance. But besides
the ordeal, less conspicuous and dramatic, but in reality
more important, is the second main aspect of initiation:
the systematic instruction of the youth in sacred myth and
tradition, the gradual unveiling of tribal mysteries and the
exhibition of sacred objects.

The ordeal and the unveiling of tribal mysteries are usually believed to have been instituted by one or more legendary ancestors or culture heroes, or by a Superior Being of superhuman character. Sometimes he is said to swallow the youths, or to kill them, and then to restore them again as fully initiated men. His voice is imitated by the hum of the bull-roarer to inspire awe in the uninitiated women and children. Through these ideas initiation brings the novice into relationship with higher powers and personalities, such as the Guardian Spirits and Tutelary Divinities of the North American Indians, the Tribal All-Father of some Australian Aborigines, the Mythological Heroes of Melanesia and other parts of the world. This is the third fundamental element, besides ordeal and the teaching of tradition, in the rites of passing into manhood.

Now what is the sociological function of these customs, what part do they play in the maintenance and development of civilization? As we have seen, the youth is taught in them the sacred traditions under most impressive conditions of preparation and ordeal and under the sanction of Supernatural Beings—the light of tribal revelation bursts upon him from out of the shadows of fear, privation, and bodily pain.

Let us realize that in primitive conditions tradition is of supreme value for the community and nothing matters as much as the conformity and conservatism of its members. Order and civilization can be maintained only by strict adhesion to the lore and knowledge received from previous generations. Any laxity in this weakens the cohesion of the group and imperils its cultural outfit to the point of threatening its very existence. Man has not yet devised the extremely complex apparatus of modern science which enables him nowadays to fix the results of experience into imperishable molds, to test it ever anew, gradually to shape it into more adequate forms and enrich it constantly by new additions. The primitive man's share of knowledge, his social fabric, his customs and beliefs, are the invaluable yield of devious experience of his forefathers, bought at an extravagant price and to be maintained at any cost. Thus, of all his qualities, truth to tradition is the most important, and a society which makes its tradition sacred has gained by it an inestimable advantage of power and permanence. Such beliefs and practices, therefore, which put a halo of sanctity round tradition and a supernatural stamp upon it, will have a "survival value" for the type of civilization in which they have been evolved.

We may, therefore, lay down the main function of initiation ceremonies: they are a ritual and dramatic expression of the supreme power and value of tradition in primitive societies; they also serve to impress this power and value upon the minds of each generation, and they are at the same time an extremely efficient means of transmitting tribal lore, of insuring continuity in tradition and of maintaining tribal cohesion.

We still have to ask: What is the relation between the purely physiological fact of bodily maturity which these ceremonies mark, and their social and religious aspect? We see at once that religion does something more, infinitely more, than the mere "sacralizing of a crisis of life." From a natural event it makes a social transition, to the fact of bodily maturity it adds the vast conception of entry into manhood with its duties, privileges, responsibilities, above all with its knowledge of tradition and the communion with sacred things and beings. There is thus a creative element in the rites of religious nature. The act establishes not only a social event in the life of the individual but also a spiritual metamorphosis, both associated with the biological event but transcending it in importance and significance.

Initiation is a typically religious act, and we can see clearly here how the ceremony and its purpose are one, how the end is realized in the very consummation of the act. At the same time we can see the function of such acts in society in that they create mental habits and social usages of inestimable value to the group and its civilization.

Another type of religious ceremony, the rite of marriage, is also an end in itself that it creates a supernaturally sanctioned bond, superadded to the primarily biological fact: the union of man and woman for lifelong partnership in affection, economic community, the procreation and rearing of children. This union, monogamous marriage, has always existed in human societies—so modern anthropology teaches in the face of the older fantastic hypotheses of "promiscuity" and "group marriage." By giving monogamous marriage an imprint of value and sanctity, religion offers another gift to human culture. And that brings us to the consideration of the two great human needs of propagation and nutrition.

2. PROVIDENCE IN PRIMITIVE LIFE Propagation and nutrition stand first and foremost among the vital concerns of man. Their relation to religious belief and practice has been often recognized and even overemphasized. Especially sex has been, from some older writers up to the psychoanalytic school, frequently regarded as the main source of religion. In fact, however, it plays an astonishingly insignificant part in religion, considering its force and insidiousness in human life in general. Besides love magic and the use of sex in certain magical performances—phenomena not belonging to the domain of religion—there remain to be mentioned here only acts of licence at harvest festivities or other public gatherings, the facts of temple prostitution and, at the level of barbarism and lower civilization, the worship of phallic divinities. Contrary to what one would expect, in savagery sexual cults play an insignificant role. It must also be remembered that acts of ceremonial licence are not mere indulgence, but that they express a reverent attitude towards the forces of generation and fertility in man and nature, forces on which the very existence of society and culture depends. Religion, the permanent source of moral control, which changes its incidence but remains eternally vigilant, has to turn its attention to these forces, at first drawing them merely into its sphere, later on submitting them to

repression, finally establishing the ideal of chastity and the
sanctification of askesis.

When we pass to nutrition, the first thing to be noted
is that eating is for primitive man an act surrounded by
etiquette, special prescriptions and prohibitions, and a
general emotional tension to a degree unknown to us. Besides the magic of food, designed to make it go a long way,
or to prevent its scarcity in general—and we do not speak
here at all of the innumerable forms of magic associated
with the procuring of food—food has also a conspicuous
role in ceremonies of a distinctly religious character. First-
fruit offerings of a ritual nature, harvest ceremonies, big
seasonal feasts in which crops are accumulated, displayed,
and, in one way or another, sacralized, play an important
part among agricultural people. Hunters, again, or fishers
celebrate a big catch or the opening of the season of their
pursuit by feasts and ceremonies at which food is ritually
handled, the animals propitiated or worshipped. All such
acts express the joy of the community, their sense of the
great value of food, and religion through them consecrates
the reverent attitude of man towards his daily bread.

To primitive man, never, even under the best conditions,
quite free from the threat of starvation, abundance of food
is a primary condition of normal life. It means the possibility of looking beyond the daily worries, of paying more
attention to the remoter, spiritual aspects of civilization. If
we thus consider that food is the main link between man
and his surroundings, that by receiving it he feels the forces
of destiny and providence, we can see the cultural, nay,
biological importance of primitive religion in the sacraliza-
tion of food. We can see in it the germs of what in higher
types of religion will develop into the feeling of dependence
upon Providence, of gratitude, and of confidence in it.

Sacrifice and communion, the two main forms in which
food is ritually ministered, can now be held in a new
light against the background of man's early attitude of religious reverence towards the providential abundance of
food. That the idea of giving, the importance of the ex-

change of gifts in all phases of social contact, plays a great role in sacrifice seems—in spite of the unpopularity of this theory nowadays—unquestionable in view of the new knowledge of primitive economic psychology.[1] Since the giving of gifts is the normal accompaniment of all social intercourse among primitives, the spirits who visit the village or the demons who haunt some hallowed spot, or divinities when approached are given their due, their share sacrificed from the general plenty, as any other visitors or persons visited would be. But underlying this custom there is a still deeper religious element. Since food is to the savage the token of the beneficence of the world, since plenty gives him the first, the most elementary, inkling of Providence, by sharing in food sacrificially with his spirits or divinities the savage shares with them in the beneficial powers of his Providence already felt by him but not yet comprehended. Thus in primitive societies the roots of sacrificial offerings are to be found in the psychology of gift, which is to the communion in beneficent abundance.

The sacramental meal is only another expression of the same mental attitude, carried out in the most appropriate manner by the act by which life is retained and renewed— the act of eating. But this ritual seems to be extremely rare among lower savages, and the sacrament of communion, prevalent at a level of culture when the primitive psychology of eating is no more, has by then acquired a different symbolic and mystical meaning. Perhaps the only case of sacramental eating, well attested and known with some detail, is the so-called "totemic sacrament" of Central Australian tribes, and this seems to require a somewhat more special interpretation.

[1] *Cf.* the writer's *Argonauts of the Western Pacific*, 1923, and the article on "Primitive Economics" in the *Economic Journal*, 1921; as well as Professor Rich. Thurnwald's memoir on "Die Gestaltung der Wirtschaftsentwicklung aus ihren Anfangen heraus" in *Erinnerungsgabe fur Max Weber*, 1923.

3. MAN'S SELECTIVE INTEREST IN NATURE This brings
us to the subject of totemism, briefly defined in the first
section. As may have been seen, the following questions
have to be asked about totemism. First, why does a primitive tribe select for its totems a limited number of species,
primarily animals and plants; and on what principles is this
selection made? Secondly, why is this selective attitude expressed in beliefs of affinity, in cults of multiplication, above
all in the negative injunctions of totemic taboos, and again
in injunctions of ritual eating, as in the Australian "totemic
sacrament"? Thirdly and finally, why with the subdivision
of nature into a limited number of selected species does
there run parallel a subdivision of the tribe into clans cor-
related with the species?

The above outlined psychology of the primitive attitude
towards food and its abundance and our principle of man's
practical and pragmatic outlook lead us directly to an answer. We have seen that food is the primary link between
the primitive and providence. And the need of it and the
desire for its abundance have led man to economic pursuits,
collecting, hunting, fishing, and they endow these pursuits
with varied and tense emotions. A number of animal and
vegetable species, those which form the staple food of the
tribe, dominate the interests of the tribesmen. To primitive
man nature is his living larder, to which—especially at
the lowest stages of culture—he has to repair directly in
order to gather, cook, and eat when hungry. The road from
the wilderness to the savage's belly and consequently to his
mind is very short, and for him the world is an indiscrimi-
nate background against which there stand out the useful,
primarily the edible, species of animals or plants. Those
who have lived in the jungle with savages, taking part in
collecting or hunting expeditions, or who have sailed with
them over the lagoons, or spent moonlit nights on sand-
banks waiting for the shoals of fish or for the appearance of
turtle, know how keen and selective is the savage's interest,

how it clings to the indications, trails, and to the habits and peculiarities of his quarry, while it yet remains quite indifferent to any other stimuli. Every such species which is habitually pursued forms a nucleus round which all the interests, the impulses, the emotions of a tribe tend to crystallize. A sentiment of social nature is built round each species, a sentiment which naturally finds its expression in folklore, belief, and ritual.

It must also be remembered that the same type of impulse which makes small children delight in birds, take a keen interest in animals, and shrink from reptiles, places animals in the front rank of nature for primitive man. By their general affinity with man—they move, utter sounds, manifest emotions, have bodies and faces like him—and by their superior powers—the birds fly in the open, the fishes swim under water, reptiles renew their skins and their life and can disappear in the earth—by all this the animal, the intermediate link between man and nature, often his superior in strength, agility, and cunning, usually his indispensable quarry, assumes an exceptional place in the savage's view of the world.

The primitive is deeply interested in the appearance and properties of beasts; he desires to have them and, therefore, to control them as useful and edible things; sometimes he admires and fears them. All these interests meet and, strengthening each other, produce the same effect: the selection, in man's principal preoccupations, of a limited number of species, animal first, vegetable in the second place, while inanimate or man-made things are unquestionably but a secondary formation, an introduction by analogy, of objects which have nothing to do with the substance of totemism.

The nature of man's interest in the totemic species indicates also clearly the type of belief and cult to be there expected. Since it is the desire to control the species, dangerous, useful, or edible, this desire must lead to a belief in special power over the species, affinity with it, a common essence between man and beast or plant. Such a belief

implies, on the one hand, certain considerations and re-
straints—the most obvious being a prohibition to kill and to
eat; on the other hand, it endows man with the supernatural
faculty of contributing ritually to the abundance of the
species, to its increase and vitality.

This ritual leads to acts of magical nature, by which
plenty is brought about. Magic, as we shall see presently,
tends in all its manifestations to become specialized, exclusive and departmental and hereditary within a family
or clan. In totemism the magical multiplication of each
species would naturally become the duty and privilege of
a specialist, assisted by his family. The families in course
of time become clans, each having its headman as the chief
magician of its totem. Totemism in its most elementary
forms, as found in Central Australia, is a system of magical
co-operation, a number of practical cults, each with its
own social basis but all having one common end: the supply
of the tribe with abundance. Thus totemism in its sociological aspect can be explained by the principles of primitive
magical sociology in general. The existence of totemic clans
and their correlation with cult and belief is but an instance
of departmental magic and of the tendency to inheritance
of magical ritual by one family. This explanation, somewhat
condensed as it is, attempts to show that, in its social organization, belief, and cult, totemism is not a freakish out-
growth, not a fortuitous result of some special accident or
constellation, but the natural outcome of natural conditions.

Thus we find our questions answered: man's selective
interest in a limited number of animals and plants and the
way in which this interest is ritually expressed and socially
conditioned appear as the natural result of primitive existence, of the savage's spontaneous attitudes towards
natural objects and of his prevalent occupations. From the
survival point of view, it is vital that man's interest in the
practically indispensable species should never abate, that
his belief in his capacity to control them should give him
strength and endurance in his pursuits and stimulate his

observation and knowledge of the habits and natures of animals and plants. Totemism appears thus as a blessing bestowed by religion on primitive man's efforts in dealing with his useful surroundings, upon his "struggle for existence." At the same time it develops his reverence for those animals and plants on which he depends, to which he feels in a way grateful, and yet the destruction of which is a necessity to him. And all this springs from the belief of man's affinity with those forces of nature upon which he mainly depends. Thus we find a moral value and a biological significance in totemism, in a system of beliefs, practices, and social arrangements which at first sight appears but a childish, irrevelant, and degrading fancy of the savage.

4. DEATH AND THE REINTEGRATION OF THE GROUP Of all sources of religion, the supreme and final crisis of life—death—is of the greatest importance. Death is the gateway to the other world in more than the literal sense. According to most theories of early religion, a great deal, if not all, of religious inspiration has been derived from it—and in this orthodox views are on the whole correct. Man has to live his life in the shadow of death, and he who clings to life and enjoys its fullness must dread the menace of its end. And he who is faced by death turns to the promise of life. Death and its denial—Immortality—have always formed, as they form today, the most poignant theme of man's forebodings. The extreme complexity of man's emotional reactions to life finds necessarily its counterpart in his attitude to death. Only what in life has been spread over a long space and manifested in a succession of experiences and events is here at its end condensed into one crisis which provokes a violent and complex outburst of religious manifestations.

Even among the most primitive peoples, the attitude towards death is infinitely more complex and, I may add, more akin to our own, than is usually assumed. It is often stated by anthropologists that the dominant feeling of the survivors is that of horror at the corpse and of fear of the ghost. This twin attitude is even made by no less an authority than Wilhelm Wundt the very nucleus of all religious belief and practice. Yet this assertion is only a half-truth, which means no truth at all. The emotions are extremely complex and even contradictory; the dominant elements, love of the dead and loathing of the corpse, passionate attachment to the personality still lingering about the body and a shattering fear of the gruesome thing that has been left over, these two elements seem to mingle and play into each other. This is reflected in the spontaneous behavior and in the ritual proceedings at death. In the tending of the corpse, in the modes of its disposal, in the post-funerary and commemorative ceremonies, the nearest relatives, the mother mourning for her son, the widow for her husband, the child for the parent, always show some horror and fear mingled with pious love, but never do the negative elements appear alone or even dominant.

The mortuary proceedings show a striking similarity throughout the world. As death approaches, the nearest relatives in any case, sometimes the whole community, forgather by the dying man, and dying, the most private act which a man can perform, is transformed into a public, tribal event. As a rule, a certain differentiation takes place at once, some of the relatives watching near the corpse, others making preparations for the pending end and its consequences, others again performing perhaps some religious acts at a sacred spot. Thus in certain parts of Melanesia the real kinsmen must keep at a distance and only relatives by marriage perform the mortuary services, while in some tribes of Australia the reverse order is observed.

As soon as death has occurred, the body is washed, anointed and adorned, sometimes the bodily apertures are filled, the arms and legs tied together. Then it is exposed to the view of all, and the most important phase, the immediate mourning begins. Those who have witnessed death and its sequel among savages and who can compare these events with their counterpart among other uncivilized peoples must be struck by the fundamental similarity of the proceedings. There is always a more or less conventionalized and dramatized outburst of grief and wailing in sorrow, which often passes among savages into bodily lacerations and the tearing of hair. This is always done in a public display and is associated with visible signs of mourning, such as black or white daubs on the body, shaven or disheveled hair, strange or torn garments.

The immediate mourning goes on round the corpse. This, far from being shunned or dreaded, is usually the center of pious attention. Often there are ritual forms of fondling or attestations of reverence. The body is sometimes kept on the knees of seated persons, stroked and embraced. At the same time these acts are usually considered both dangerous and repugnant, duties to be fulfilled at some cost to the performer. After a time the corpse has to be disposed of. Inhumation with an open or closed grave; exposure in caves or on platforms, in hollow trees or on the ground in some wild desert place; burning or setting adrift in canoes—these are the usual forms of disposal.

This brings us to perhaps the most important point, the two-fold contradictory tendency, on the one hand to preserve the body, to keep its form intact, or to retain parts of it; on the other hand the desire to be done with it, to put it out of the way, to annihilate it completely. Mummification and burning are the two extreme expressions of this two-fold tendency. It is impossible to regard mummification or burning or any intermediate form as determined by mere accident of belief, as a historical feature of some culture or other which has gained its universality by the mechanism of spread and contact only. For in these customs is clearly expressed the fundamental attitude of mind of the surviving relative, friend or lover, the longing for all that remains of the dead person and the disgust and fear of the dreadful transformation wrought by death.

One extreme and interesting variety in which this double-

edged attitude is expressed in a gruesome manner is sarco-
cannibalism, a custom of partaking in piety of the flesh of
the dead person. It is done with extreme repugnance and
dread and usually followed by a violent vomiting fit. At
the same time it is felt to be a supreme act of reverence,
love, and devotion. In fact it is considered such a sacred
duty that among the Melanesians of New Guinea, where
I have studied and witnessed it, it is still performed in
secret, although severely penalized by the white Government. The smearing of the body with the fat of the dead,
prevalent in Australia and Papuasia is, perhaps, but a variety
of this custom.

In all such rites, there is a desire to maintain the tie
and the parallel tendency to break the bond. Thus the
funerary rites are considered as unclean and soiling, the
contact with the corpse as defiling and dangerous, and the
performers have to wash, cleanse their body, remove all
traces of contact, and perform ritual lustrations. Yet the
mortuary ritual compels man to overcome the repugnance,
to conquer his fears, to make piety and attachment trium-
phant, and with it the belief in a future life, in the survival
of the spirit.

And here we touch on one of the most important functions of religious cult. In the foregoing analysis I have laid
stress on the direct emotional forces created by contact with
death and with the corpse, for they primarily and most
powerfully determine the behavior of the survivors. But
connected with these emotions and born out of them, there
is the idea of the spirit, the belief in the new life into which
the departed has entered. And here we return to the problem of animism with which we began our survey of primitive religious facts. What is the substance of a spirit, and
what is the psychological origin of this belief?

The savage is intensely afraid of death, probably as the
result of some deep-seated instincts common to man and
animals. He does not want to realize it as an end, he cannot
face the idea of complete cessation, of annihilation. The
idea of spirit and of spiritual existence is near at hand,

furnished by such experiences as are discovered and described by Tylor. Grasping at it, man reaches the comforting belief in spiritual continuity and in the life after death. Yet this belief does not remain unchallenged in the complex, double-edged play of hope and fear which sets in always in the face of death. To the comforting voice of hope, to the intense desire of immortality, to the difficulty, in one's own case, almost the impossibility, of facing annihilation there are opposed powerful and terrible forebodings. The testimony of the senses, the gruesome decomposition of the corpse, the visible disappearance of the personality—certain apparently instinctive suggestions of fear and horror seem to threaten man at all stages of culture with some idea of annihilation, with some hidden fears and forebodings. And here into this play of emotional forces, into this supreme dilemma of life and final death, religion steps in, selecting the positive creed, the comforting view, the culturally valuable belief in immortality, in the spirit independent of the body, and in the continuance of life after death. In the various ceremonies at death, in commemoration and communion with the departed, and worship of ancestral ghosts, religion gives body and form to the saving beliefs.

Thus the belief in immortality is the result of a deep emotional revelation, standardized by religion, rather than a primitive philosophic doctrine. Man's conviction of continued life is one of the supreme gifts of religion, which judges and selects the better of the two alternatives suggested by self-preservation—the hope of continued life and the fear of annihilation. The belief in spirits is the result of the belief in immortality. The substance of which the spirits are made is the full-blooded passion and desire for life, rather than the shadowy stuff which haunts his dreams and illusions. Religion saves man from a surrender to death and destruction, and in doing this it merely makes use of the observations of dreams, shadows, and visions. The real nucleus of animism lies in the deepest emotional fact of human nature, the desire for life.

Thus the rites of mourning, the ritual behavior imme-
diately after death, can be taken as pattern of the religious
act, while the belief in immortality, in the continuity of
life and in the nether world, can be taken as the prototype
of an act of faith. Here, as in the religious ceremonies pre-
viously described, we find self-contained acts, the aim of
which is achieved in their very performance. The ritual
despair, the obsequies, the acts of mourning, express the
emotion of the bereaved and the loss of the whole group.
They endorse and they duplicate the natural feelings of
the survivors; they create a social event out of a natural
fact. Yet, though in the acts of mourning, in the mimic
despair of wailing, in the treatment of the corpse and in
its disposal, nothing ulterior is achieved, these acts fulfill
an important function and possess a considerable value for
primitive culture.

What is this function? The initiation ceremonies we have
found fulfill theirs in sacralizing tradition; the food cults,
sacrament and sacrifice bring man into communion with
providence, with the beneficent forces of plenty; totemism
standardizes man's practical, useful attitude of selective
interest towards his surroundings. If the view here taken of
the biological function of religion is true, some such similar
role must also be played by the whole mortuary ritual.

The death of a man or woman in a primitive group, consisting of a limited number of individuals, is an event of no
mean importance. The nearest relatives and friends are
disturbed to the depth of their emotional life. A small community bereft of a member, especially if he be important,
is severely mutilated. The whole event breaks the normal
course of life and shakes the moral foundations of society.
The strong tendency on which we have insisted in the above
description: to give way to fear and horror, to abandon the
corpse, to run away from the village, to destroy all the be-
longings of the dead one—all these impulses exist, and if
given way to would be extremely dangerous, disintegrating
the group, destroying the material foundations of primitive
culture. Death in a primitive society is, therefore, much

more than the removal of a member. By setting in motion one part of the deep forces of the instinct of self-preservation, it threatens the very cohesion and solidarity of the group, and upon this depends the organization of that society, its tradition, and finally the whole culture. For if primitive man yielded always to the disintegrating impulses of his reaction to death, the continuity of tradition and the existence of material civilization would be made impossible.

We have seen already how religion, by sacralizing and thus standardizing the other set of impulses, bestows on man the gift of mental integrity. Exactly the same function it fulfills also with regard to the whole group. The ceremonial of death which ties the survivors to the body and rivets them to the place of death, the beliefs in the existence of the spirit, in its beneficent influences or malevolent intentions, in the duties of a series of commemorative or sacrificial ceremonies—in all this religion counteracts the centrifugal forces of fear, dismay, demoralization, and provides the most powerful means of reintegration of the group's shaken solidarity and of the re-establishment of its morale.

In short, religion here assures the victory of tradition and culture over the mere negative response of thwarted instinct.

With the rites of death we have finished the survey of the main types of religious acts. We have followed the crises of life as the main guiding thread of our account, but as they presented themselves we also treated the side issues, such as totemism, the cults of food and of propagation, sacrifice and sacrament, the commemorative cults of ancestors and the cults of the spirits. To one type already mentioned we still have to return—I mean, the seasonal feasts and ceremonies of communal or tribal character—and to the discussion of this subject we proceed now.

IV. THE PUBLIC AND TRIBAL CHARACTER OF
PRIMITIVE CULTS

The festive and public character of the ceremonies of cult is a conspicuous feature of religion in general. Most sacred acts happen in a congregation; indeed, the solemn conclave of the faithful united in prayer, sacrifice, supplication, or thanksgiving is the very prototype of a religious ceremony. Religion needs the community as a whole so that its members may worship in common its sacred things and its divinities, and society needs religion for the maintenance of moral law and order.

In primitive societies the public character of worship, the give-and-take between religious faith and social organization, is at least as pronounced as in higher cultures. It is sufficient to glance over our previous inventory of religious phenomena to see that ceremonies at birth, rites of initiation, mortuary attentions to the dead, burial, the acts of mourning and commemoration, sacrifice and totemic ritual, are one and all public and collective, frequently affecting the tribe as a whole and absorbing all its energies for the time being. This public character, the gathering together of big numbers, is especially pronounced in the annual or periodical feasts held at times of plenty, at harvest or at the height of the hunting or fishing season. Such feasts allow the people to indulge in their gay mood, to enjoy the abundance of crops and quarry, to meet their friends and relatives, to muster the whole community in full force, and to do all this in a mood of happiness and harmony. At times during such festivals visits of the departed take place: the spirits of ancestors and dead relatives return and receive offerings and sacrificial libations, mingle with the survivors in the acts of cult and in the rejoicings of the feast. Or the dead, even if they do not actually revisit the survivors, are commemorated by them, usually in the form of ancestor cult. Again, such festivities being frequently held, embody the ritual of garnered crops and other cults of vegetation. But whatever the other issues of such festivities, there can be no doubt that religion demands the existence of seasonal, periodical feasts with a big concourse of people, with rejoicings and festive apparel, with an abundance of food, and with relaxation of rules and taboos. The members of the tribe come together, and they relax the usual restrictions, especially the barriers of conventional reserve in social and in sexual intercourse. The appetites are provided for, indeed pandered to, and there is a common participation in the pleasures, a display to everyone of all that is good, the sharing of it in a universal mood of generosity. To the interest in plenty of material goods there is joined the interest in the multitude of people, in the congregation, in the tribe as a body.

With these facts of periodical festive gathering a number of other distinctly social elements must be ranged: the tribal character of almost all religious ceremonies, the social universality of moral rules, the contagion of sin, the importance of sheer convention and tradition in primitive religion and morals, above all the identification of the whole tribe as a social unit with its religion; that is, the absence of any religious sectarianism, dissention, or heterodoxy in primitive creed.

1. SOCIETY AS THE SUBSTANCE OF GOD All these facts, especially the last one, show that religion is a tribal affair, and we are reminded of the famous dictum of Robertson Smith, that primitive religion is the concern of the community rather than of the individual. This exaggerated view contains a great deal of truth, but, in science, to recognize where the truth lies, on the one hand, and to unearth it and bring it fully to light, on the other, are by no means the same. Robertson Smith did not do much more in this matter, in fact, than set forth the important problem: why is it that primitive man performs his ceremonies in public?

What is the relation between society and the truth revealed by religion and worshipped in it?

To these questions, some modern anthropologists, as we know, give a trenchant, apparently conclusive, and exceedingly simple answer. Professor Durkheim and his followers maintain that religion is social for all its Entities, its God or Gods, the Stuff all things religious are made of, are nothing more nor less than Society divinized.

This theory seems very well to explain the public nature of cult, the inspiration and comfort drawn by man, the social animal, from congregation, the intolerance shown by religion, especially in its early manifestations, the cogency of morals and other similar facts. It also satisfies our modern democratic bias, which in social science appears as a tendency to explain all by "collective" rather than by "individual forces." This, the theory which makes vox *populi* vox *Dei* appear as a sober, scientific truth, must surely be congenial to modern man.

Yet, upon reflection, critical misgivings, and very serious ones at that, arise. Everyone who has experienced religion deeply and sincerely knows that the strongest religious moments come in solitude, in turning away from the world, in concentration and in mental detachment, and not in the distraction of a crowd. Can primitive religion be so entirely devoid of the inspiration of solitude? No one who knows savages at firsthand or from a careful study of literature will have any doubts. Such facts as the seclusion of novices at initiation, their individual, personal struggles during the ordeal, the communion with spirits, divinities, and powers in lonely spots, all these show us primitive religion frequently lived through in solitude. Again, as we have seen before, the belief in immortality cannot be explained without the consideration of the religious frame of mind of the individual, who faces his own pending death in fear and sorrow. Primitive religion does not entirely lack its prophets, seers, soothsayers and interpreters of belief. All such facts, though they certainly do not prove that religion is exclusively individual, make it difficult to understand how it can be regarded as *the Social* pure and simple.

And again, the essence of morals, as opposed to legal or customary rules, is that they are enforced by conscience. The savage does not keep his taboo for fear of social punishment or of public opinion. He abstains from breaking it partly because he fears the direct evil consequences flowing from the will of a divinity, or from the forces of the sacred, but mainly because his personal responsibility and conscience forbid him doing it. The forbidden totem animal, incestuous or forbidden intercourse, the tabooed action or food, are directly abhorrent to him. I have seen and felt savages shrink from an illicit action with the same horror and disgust with which the religious Christian will shrink from the committing of what he considers sin. Now this mental attitude is undoubtedly due in part to the influence of society, in so far as the particular prohibition is branded as horrible and disgusting by tradition. But it works in the individual and through forces of the individual mind. It is, therefore, neither exclusively social nor individual, but a mixture of both.

Professor Durkheim tries to establish his striking theory that Society is the raw material of Godhead by an analysis of primitive tribal festivities. He studies especially the seasonal ceremonies of the Central Australians. In these "the great collective effervescence during the periods of concentration" causes all the phenomena of their religion, and "the religious idea is born out of their effervescence." Professor Durkheim lays thus the emphasis on emotional ebullition, on exaltation, on the increased power which every individual feels when part of such a gathering. Yet but a little reflection is sufficient to show that even in primitive societies the heightening of emotions and the lifting of the individual out of himself are by no means restricted to gatherings and to crowd phenomena. The lover near his sweetheart, the daring adventurer conquering his fears in the face of real danger, the hunter at grips with a wild animal, the craftsman achieving a masterpiece, whether he

be savage or civilized, will under such conditions feel al-
tered, uplifted, endowed with higher forces. And there can
be no doubt that from many of these solitary experiences
where man feels the forebodings of death, the pangs of
anxiety, the exaltation of bliss, there flows a great deal of
religious inspiration. Though most ceremonies are carried
out in public, much of religious revelation takes place in
solitude.

On the other hand there are in primitive societies collective acts with as much effervescence and passion as any
religious ceremony can possibly have, yet without the
slightest religious coloring. Collective work in the gardens,
as I have seen it in Melanesia, when men become carried
away with emulation and zest for work, singing rhythmic
songs, uttering shouts of joy and slogans of competitive
challenge, is full of this "collective effervescence." But it is
entirely profane, and society which "reveals itself" in this as
in any other public performance assumes no divine grandeur or godlike appearance. A battle, a sailing regatta, one
of the big tribal gatherings for trading purposes, an Australian lay-corrobboree, a village brawl, are all from the social
as well as from the psychological point of view essentially
examples of crowd effervescence. Yet no religion is gener-
ated on any of these occasions. Thus the *collective* and the
religious, though impinging on each other, are by no means
coextensive, and while a great deal of belief and religious
inspiration must be traced back to solitary experiences of
man, there is much concourse and effervescence which has
no religious meaning or religious consequence.

If we extend yet further the definition of "society" and
regard it as a permanent entity, continuous through tradition and culture, each generation brought up by its pred-
ecessor and molded into its likeness by the social heritage
of civilization—can we not regard then Society as the prototype of Godhead? Even thus the facts of primitive life will
remain rebellious to this theory. For tradition comprises
the sum total of social norms and customs, rules of art and
knowledge, injunctions, precepts, legends and myths, and

part of this only is religious, while the rest is essentially profane. As we have seen in the second section of this essay, primitive man's empirical and rational knowledge of nature, which is the foundation of his arts and crafts, of his economic enterprises and of his constructive abilities, forms an autonomous domain of social tradition. Society as the keeper of lay tradition, of the profane, cannot be the religious principle or Divinity, for the place of this latter is within the domain of the sacred only. We have found, moreover, that one of the chief tasks of primitive religion, especially in the performance of initiation ceremonies and tribal mysteries, is to sacralize the religious part of tradition. It is clear, therefore, that religion cannot derive all its sanctity from that source which itself is made sacred by religion.

It is in fact only by a clever play on words and by a double-edged sophistication of the argument that "society" can be identified with the Divine and the Sacred. If, indeed, we set equal the *social* to the *moral* and widen this concept so that it covers all belief, all rules of conduct, all dictates of conscience; if, further, we personify the Moral Force and regard it as a Collective Soul, then the identification of Society with Godhead needs not much dialectical skill to be defended. But since the moral rules are only one part of the traditional heritage of man, since morality is not identical with the Power of Being from which it is believed to spring, since finally the metaphysical concept of "Collective Soul" is barren in anthropology, we have to reject the sociological theory of religion.

To sum up, the views of Durkheim and his school cannot be accepted. First of all, in primitive societies religion arises to a great extent from purely individual sources. Secondly, society as a crowd is by no means always given to the production of religious beliefs or even to religious states of mind, while collective effervescence is often of an entirely secular nature. Thirdly, tradition, the sum total of certain rules and cultural achievements, embraces, and in primitive societies keeps in a tight grip, both Profane and Sacred. Finally, the personification of society, the conception of a "Collective Soul," is without any foundation in fact, and is against the sound methods of social science.

2. THE MORAL EFFICIENCY OF SAVAGE BELIEFS   With all this, in order to do justice to Robertson Smith, Durkheim, and their school, we have to admit that they have brought out a number of relevant features of primitive religion. Above all, by the very exaggeration of the sociological aspect of primitive faith they have set forth a number of most important questions: Why are most religious acts in primitive societies performed collectively and in public? What is the part of society in the establishment of the rules of moral conduct? Why are not only morality but also belief, mythology, and all sacred tradition compulsory to all the members of a primitive tribe? In other words, why is there only one body of religious beliefs in each tribe, and why is no difference of opinion ever tolerated?

To give an answer to these questions we have to go back to our survey of religious phenomena, to recall some of our conclusions there arrived at, and especially to fix our attention upon the technique by which belief is expressed and morals established in primitive religion.

Let us start with the religious act par excellence, the ceremonial of death. Here the call to religion arises out of an individual crisis, the death which threatens man or woman. Never does an individual need the comfort of belief and ritual so much as in the sacrament of the viaticum, in the last comforts given to him at the final stage of his life's journey—acts which are well-nigh universal in all primitive religions. These acts are directed against the overwhelming fear, against the corroding doubt, from which the savage is no more free than the civilized man. These acts confirm his hope that there is a hereafter, that it is not worse than present life; indeed, better. All the ritual expresses that belief, that emotional attitude which the dying man requires, which is the greatest comfort he can have in his supreme conflict. And this affirmation has behind it weight of numbers and the pomp of solemn ritual. For in all savage societies, death, as we have seen, compels the whole community to forgather, to attend to the dying, and to carry out the duties towards him. These duties do not, of course, develop any emotional sympathy with the dying —this would lead merely to a disintegrating panic. On the contrary, the line of ritual conduct opposes and contradicts some of the strongest emotions to which the dying man might become a prey. The whole conduct of the group, in fact, expresses the hope of salvation and immortality; that is, it expresses only one among the conflicting emotions of the individual.

After death, though the main actor has made his exit, the tragedy is not at an end. There are the bereaved ones, and these, savage or civilized, suffer alike, and are thrown into a dangerous mental chaos. We have given an analysis of this already, and found that, torn between fear and piety, reverence and horror, love and disgust, they are in a state of mind which might lead to mental disintegration. Out of this, religion lifts the individual by what could be called spiritual co-operation in the sacred mortuary rites. We have seen that in these rites there is expressed the dogma of continuity after death, as well as the moral attitude towards the departed. The corpse, and with it the person of the dead one, is a potential object of horror as well as of tender love. Religion confirms the second part of this double attitude by making the dead body into an object of sacred duties. The bond of union between the recently dead and the survivors is maintained, a fact of immense importance for the continuity of culture and for the safe keeping of tradition. In all this we see that the whole community carries out the biddings of religious tradition, but that these are again enacted for the benefit of a few individuals only, the bereaved ones, that they arise from a personal conflict and are a solution of this conflict. It must also be remembered that what the survivor goes through on such an occasion prepares him for his own death. The belief in immortality, which he has lived through and practiced in the case of his mother or father, makes him realize more clearly his own future life.

In all this we have to make a clear distinction between the belief and the ethics of the ritual on the one hand, and on the other the means of enforcing them, the technique by which the individual is made to receive his religious comfort. The saving belief in spiritual continuity after death is already contained in the individual mind; it is not created by society. The sum total of innate tendencies, known usually as "the instinct of self-preservation," is at the root of this belief. The faith in immortality is, as we have seen, closely connected with the difficulty of facing one's own annihilation or that of a near and beloved person. This tendency makes the idea of the final disappearance of human personality odious, intolerable, socially destructive. Yet this idea and the fear of it always lurk in individual experience, and religion can remove it only by its negation in ritual.

Whether this is achieved by a Providence directly guiding human history, or by a process of natural selection in which a culture which evolves a belief and a ritual of immortality will survive and spread—this is a problem of theology or metaphysics. The anthropologist has done enough when he has shown the value of a certain phenomenon for social integrity and for the continuity of culture. In any case we see that what religion does in this matter is to select one out of the two alternatives suggested to man by his instinctive endowment.

This selection once made, however, society is indispensable for its enactment. The bereaved member of the group, himself overwhelmed by sorrow and fear, is incapable of relying on his own forces. He would be unable by his single effort to apply the dogma to his own case. Here the group steps in. The other members, untouched by the calamity, not torn mentally by the metaphysical dilemma, can respond to the crisis along the lines dictated by the religious order. Thus they bring consolation to the stricken one and lead him through the comforting experiences of religious ceremony. It is always easy to bear the misfortunes—of others, and the whole group, in which the majority are untouched by the pangs of fear and horror, can thus help the afflicted minority. Going through the religious ceremonies, the bereaved emerges changed by the revelation of immortality, communion with the beloved, the order of the next world. Religion commands in acts of cult, the group executes the command.

But, as we have seen, the comfort of ritual is not artificial, not manufactured for the occasion. It is but the result of the two conflicting tendencies which exist in man's innate emotional reaction to death: the religious attitude consists merely in the selection and ritual affirmation of one of these alternatives—the hope in a future life. And here the public concourse gives the emphasis, the powerful testimony to the belief. Public pomp and ceremony take effect through the contagiousness of faith, through the dignity of unanimous consent, the impressiveness of collective behavior. A multitude enacting as one an earnest and dignified ceremony invariably carries away even the disinterested observer, still more the affected participant.

But the distinction between social collaboration as the only technique necessary for the enactment of a belief on the one hand, and the creation of the belief or self-revelation of society on the other, must be emphatically pointed out. The community proclaims a number of definite truths and gives moral comfort to its members, but it does not give them the vague and empty assertion of its own divinity.

In another type of religious ritual, in the ceremonies of initiation, we found that the ritual establishes the existence of some power or personality from which tribal law is derived, and which is responsible for the moral rules imparted to the novice. To make the belief impressive, strong, and grandiose, there is the pomp of the ceremony and the hardships of preparation and ordeal. An unforgettable experience, unique in the life of the individual, is created, and by this he learns the doctrines of tribal tradition and the rules of its morality. The whole tribe is mobilized and all its authority set in motion to bear witness to the power and reality of the things revealed.

Here again, as at the death, we have to do with a crisis in the individual life, and a mental conflict associated with it. At puberty, the youth has to test his physical power, to cope with his sexual maturity, to take up his place in the tribe. This brings him promises, prerogatives, and temptations, and at the same time imposes burdens upon him. The right solution of the conflict lies in his compliance with tradition, in his submission to the sexual morality of his tribe and to the burdens of manhood, and that is accomplished in the ceremonies of initiation.

The public character of these ceremonies avails both to establish the greatness of the ultimate lawgiver and to achieve homogeneity and uniformity in the teaching of morals. Thus they become a form of condensed education of a religious character. As in all schooling, the principles imparted are merely selected, fixed, emphasized out of what there is in the individual endowment. Here again publicity is a matter of technique, while the contents of what is taught are not invented by society but exist in the individual.

In other cults again, such as harvest festivals, totemic gatherings, first-fruit offerings and ceremonial display of food, we find religion sacralizing abundance and security and establishing the attitude of reverence towards the beneficent forces without. Here again the publicity of the cult is necessary as the only technique suitable for the establishment of the value of food, accumulation and abundance. The display to all, the admiration of all, the rivalry between any two producers, are the means by which value is created. For every value, religious and economic, must possess universal currency. But here again we find only the selection and emphasis of one of the two possible individual reactions. Accumulated food can either be squandered or preserved. It can either be an incentive to immediate heedless consumption and light-hearted carelessness about the future, or else it can stimulate man to devising means of hoarding the treasure and of using it for culturally higher purposes. Religion sets its stamp on the culturally valuable attitude and enforces it by public enactment.

The public character of such feasts subserves another sociologically important function. The members of every group which forms a cultural unit must come in contact with each other from time to time, but besides its beneficent possibility, of strengthening social ties, such contact is also fraught with the danger of friction. The danger is greater when people meet in times of stress, dearth, and hunger, when their appetite is unsatisfied and their sexual desires ready to flare up. A festive tribal gathering at times of plenty, when everyone is in a mood of harmony with nature and consequently with each other, takes on, therefore, the character of a meeting in a moral atmosphere. I mean an atmosphere of general harmony and benevolence. The occurrence of occasional licence at such gatherings and the relaxation of the rules of sex and of certain strictures of etiquette are probably due to the same course. All motives for quarrel and disagreement must be eliminated or else a big tribal gathering could not peacefully come to an end. The moral value of harmony and good will is thus shown to be higher than the mere negative taboos which curb the principal human instincts. There is no virtue higher than charity, and in primitive religions as well as in higher it covers a multitude of sins; nay, it outweighs them.

It is, perhaps, unnecessary to go in detail over all the other types of religious acts. Totemism, the religion of the clan, which affirms the common descent from or affinity with the totemic animal, and claims the clan's collective power to control its supply and impresses upon all the clan members a joint totemic taboo and a reverential attitude towards the totemic species, must obviously culminate in public ceremonies and have a distinctly social character. Ancestor cult, the aim of which is to unite into one band of worshippers the family, the sib or the tribe, must bring them together in public ceremonies by its very nature, or else it would fail to fulfill its function. Tutelary spirits of local groups, tribes, or cities; departmental gods; professional or local divinities must one and all—by their very definition—be worshipped by village, tribe, town, profession, or body politic.

In cults which stand on the borderline between magic and religion, such as the Intichuma ceremonies, public garden rites, ceremonies of fishing and hunting, the necessity of performance in public is obvious, for these ceremonies, clearly distinguishable from any practical activities which they inaugurate or accompany, are yet their counterpart. To the co-operation in practical enterprise there corresponds the ceremony in common. Only by uniting the group of workers in an act of worship do they fulfill their cultural function.

In fact, instead of going concretely into all the types of religious ceremony, we might have established our thesis by an abstract argument: since religion centers round vital acts, and since all these command public interest of joint co-operative groups, every religious ceremony must be public and carried out by groups. All crises of life, all important enterprises, arouse the public interest of primitive communities, and they have all their ceremonies, magical or religious. The same social body of men which unites for the enterprise or is brought together by the critical event performs also the ceremonial act. Such an abstract argument, however, correct though it be, would not have allowed us to get a real insight into the mechanism of public enactment of religious acts such as we have gained by our concrete description.

3. SOCIAL AND INDIVIDUAL CONTRIBUTIONS IN PRIMITIVE RELIGION We are forced therefore to the conclusion that publicity is the indispensable technique of religious revelation in primitive communities, but that society is neither the author of religious truths, nor still less its self-revealed subject. The necessity of the public *mise en scène* of dogma

and collective enunciation of moral truths is due to several causes. Let us sum them up.

First of all, social co-operation is needed to surround the unveiling of things sacred and of supernatural beings with solemn grandeur. The community whole-heartedly engaged in performing the forms of the ritual creates the atmosphere of homogeneous belief. In this collective action, those who at the moment least need the comfort of belief, the affirmation of the truth, help along those who are in need of it. The evil, disintegrating forces of destiny are thus distributed by a system of mutual insurance in spiritual misfortune and stress. In bereavement, at the crisis of puberty, during impending danger and evil, at times when prosperity might be used well or badly—religion standardizes the right way of thinking and acting and society takes up the verdict and repeats it in unison.

In the second place, public performance of religious dogma is indispensable for the maintenance of morals in primitive communities. Every article of faith, as we have seen, wields a moral influence. Now morals, in order to be active at all, must be universal. The endurance of social ties, the mutuality of services and obligations, the possibility of co-operation, are based in any society on the fact that every member knows what is expected of him; that, in short, there is a universal standard of conduct. No rule of morals can work unless it is anticipated and unless it can be counted upon. In primitive societies, where law, as enforced by judgments and penalties, is almost completely absent, the automatic, self-acting moral rule is of the greatest importance for forming the very foundations of primitive organization and culture. This is possible only in a society where there is no private teaching of morals, no personal codes of conduct and honor, no ethical schools, no differences of moral opinion. The teaching of morals must be open, public, and universal.

Thirdly and finally, the transmission and the conservation of sacred tradition entails publicity, or at least collectiveness of performance. It is essential to every religion that its dogma should be considered and treated as absolutely inalterable and inviolable. The believer must be firmly convinced that what he is led to accept as truth is held in safekeeping, handed on exactly as it has been received, placed above any possibility of falsification or alteration. Every religion must have its tangible, reliable safeguards by which the authenticity of its tradition is guaranteed. In higher religions, we know the extreme importance of the authenticity of holy writings, the supreme concern about the purity of the text and the truth of interpretation. The native races have to rely on human memory. Yet, without books or inscriptions, without bodies of theologians, they are not less concerned about the purity of their texts, not less well safeguarded against alteration and misstatement. There is only one factor which can prevent the constant breaking of the sacred thread: the participation of a number of people in the safekeeping of tradition. The public enactment of myth among certain tribes, the official recitals of sacred stories on certain occasions, the embodiment of parts of belief in sacred ceremonies, the guardianship of parts of tradition given to special bodies of men: secret societies, totemic clans, highest-age grades—all these are means of safeguarding the doctrine of primitive religions. We see that wherever this doctrine is not quite public in the tribe there is a special type of social organization serving the purpose of its keeping.

These considerations explain also the orthodoxy of primitive religions, and excuse their intolerance. In a primitive community, not only the morals but also the dogmas have to be identical for all members. As long as savage creeds have been regarded as idle superstitions, as make-believe, as childish or diseased fancies, or at best crude philosophic speculations, it was difficult to understand why the savage clung to them so obstinately, so faithfully. But once we see that every canon of the savage's belief is a live force to him, that his doctrine is the very cement of social fabric—for all his morality is derived from it, all his social cohesion and his mental composure—it is easy to understand that he cannot afford to be tolerant. And it is clear also that once you begin to play ducks and drakes with his "superstitions," you destroy all his morality, without much chance of giving him another instead.

We see thus clearly the need for the prominently overt and collective nature of religious acts and for the universality of moral principles, and we also realize clearly why this is much more prominent in primitive religions than in civilized ones. Public participation and social interest in matters religious are thus explicable by clear, concrete, empirical reasons, and there is no room for an Entity, revealing itself in artful disguise to its worshippers, mystified and misled in the very act of revelation. The fact is that the social share in religious enactment is a condition necessary but not sufficient, and that without the analysis of the individual mind, we cannot take one step in the understanding of religion.

At the beginning of our survey of religious phenomena, in Section III, we have made a distinction between magic and religion; later on in the account, however, we left the magical rites completely on one side, and to this important domain of primitive life we have now to return.

V. THE ART OF MAGIC AND THE POWER OF FAITH

Magic—the very word seems to reveal a world of mysterious and unexpected possibilities! Even for those who do not share in that hankering after the occult, after the short cuts into "esoteric truth," this morbid interest, nowadays so freely ministered to by stale revivals of half-understood ancient creeds and cults, dished up under the names of "theosophy," "spiritism" or "spiritualism," and various pseudo-"sciences," -ologies and -isms—even for the clear scientific mind the subject of magic has a special attraction. Partly perhaps because we hope to find in it the quintessence of primitive man's longings and of his wisdom—and that, whatever it might be, is worth knowing. Partly because "magic" seems to stir up in everyone some hidden mental forces, some lingering hopes in the miraculous, some dormant beliefs in man's mysterious possibilities. Witness to this is the power which the words *magic, spell, charm, to bewitch,* and *to enchant,* possess in poetry, where the inner value of words, the emotional forces which they still release, survive longest and are revealed most clearly.

Yet when the sociologist approaches the study of magic, there where it still reigns supreme, where even now it can be found fully developed—that is, among the Stone Age savages of today—he finds to his disappointment an entirely sober, prosaic, even clumsy art, enacted for purely practical reasons, governed by crude and shallow beliefs, carried out in a simple and monotonous technique. This was already indicated in the definition of magic given above when in order to distinguish it from religion we described it as a body of purely practical acts, performed as a means to an end. Such also we have found it when we tried to disentangle it from knowledge and from practical arts, in which it is so strongly enmeshed, superficially so alike that it requires some effort to distinguish the essentially different mental attitude and the specifically ritual nature of its acts. Primitive magic—every field anthropologist knows it to his cost—is extremely monotonous and unexciting, strictly limited in its means of action, circumscribed in its beliefs, stunted in its fundamental assumptions. Follow one rite, study one spell, grasp the principles of magical belief, art and sociology in one case, and you will know not only all the acts of the tribe, but, adding a variant here and there, you will be able to settle as a magical practitioner in any part of the world yet fortunate enough to have faith in that desirable art.

1. THE RITE AND THE SPELL   Let us have a look at a typical act of magic, and choose one which is well-known and generally regarded as a standard performance—an act of black magic. Among the several types which we meet in

savagery, witchcraft by the act of pointing the magical dart
is, perhaps, the most widespread of all. A pointed bone or
a stick, an arrow or the spine of some animal, is ritually, in
a mimic fashion, thrust, thrown, or pointed in the direction
of the man to be killed by sorcery. We have innumerable
recipes in the oriental and ancient books of magic, in
ethnographic descriptions and tales of travelers, of how
such a rite is performed. But the emotional setting, the
gestures and expressions of the sorcerer during the performance, have been but seldom described. Yet these are
of the greatest importance. If a spectator were suddenly
transported to some part of Melanesia and could observe
the sorcerer at work, not perhaps knowing exactly what he
was looking at, he might think that he had either to do
with a lunatic or else he would guess that here was a man
acting under the sway of uncontrolled anger. For the
sorcerer has, as an essential part of the ritual performance,
not merely to point the bone dart at his victim, but with an
intense expression of fury and hatred he has to thrust it in
the air, turn and twist it as if to bore it in the wound, then
pull it back with a sudden jerk. Thus not only is the act of
violence, or stabbing, reproduced, but the passion of violence has to be enacted.

We see thus that the dramatic expression of emotion is
the essence of this act, for what is it that is reproduced in
it? Not its end, for the magician would in that case have to
imitate the death of the victim, but the emotional state of
the performer, a state which closely corresponds to the situation in which we find it and which has to be gone through
mimetically.

I could adduce a number of similar rites from my own
experience, and many more, of course, from other records.
Thus, when in other types of black magic the sorcerer
ritually injures or mutilates or destroys a figure or object
symbolizing the victim, this rite is, above all, a clear expression of hatred and anger. Or when in love magic the
performer has really or symbolically to grasp, stroke, fondle
the beloved person or some object representing her, he

reproduces the behavior of a heartsick lover who has lost his common sense and is overwhelmed by passion. In war magic, anger, the fury of attack, the emotions of combative passion, are frequently expressed in a more or less direct manner. In the magic of terror, in the exorcism directed against powers of darkness and evil, the magician behaves as if himself overcome by the emotion of fear, or at least violently struggling against it. Shouts, brandishing of weapons, the use of lighted torches, form often the substance of this rite. Or else in an act, recorded by myself, to ward off the evil powers of darkness, a man has ritually to tremble, to utter a spell slowly as if paralyzed by fear. And this fear gets hold also of the approaching sorcerer and wards him off.

All such acts, usually rationalized and explained by some principle of magic, are *prima facie* expressions of emotion. The substances and paraphernalia used in them have often the same significance. Daggers, sharp-pointed lacerating objects, evil-smelling or poisonous substances, used in black magic; scents, flowers, inebriating stimulants, in love magic; valuables, in economic magic—all these are associated primarily through emotions and not through ideas with the end of the respective magic.

Besides such rites, however, in which a dominant element serves to express an emotion, there are others in which the act does forecast its result, or, to use Sir James Frazer's expression, the rite imitates its end. Thus, in the black magic of the Melanesians recorded by myself, a characteristic ritual way of winding-up the spell is for the sorcerer to weaken the voice, utter a death rattle, and fall down in imitation of the rigor of death. It is, however, not necessary to adduce any other examples, for this aspect of magic and the allied one of contagious magic has been brilliantly described and exhaustively documented by Frazer. Sir James has also shown that there exists a special lore of magical substances based on affinities, relations, on ideas of similarity and contagion, developed with a magical pseudo-science.

But there are also ritual proceedings in which there is neither imitation nor forecasting nor the expression of any special idea or emotion. There are rites so simple that they can be described only as an immediate application of magical virtue, as when the performer stands up and, directly invoking the wind, causes it to rise. Or again, as when a man conveys the spell to some material substance which afterwards will be applied to the thing or person to be charmed. The material objects used in such ritual are also of a strictly appropriate character—substances best fitted to receive, retain, and transmit magical virtue, coverings designed to imprison and preserve it until it is applied to its object.

But what is the magical virtue which figures not only in the last-mentioned type of act but in every magical rite? For whether it be an act expressing certain emotions or a rite of imitation and foreshadowing or an act of simple casting, one feature they have always in common: the force of magic, its virtue, must always be conveyed to the charmed object. What is it? Briefly, it is always the power contained in the spell, for, and this is never sufficiently emphasized, the most important element in magic is the spell. The spell is that part of magic which is occult, handed over in magical filiation, known only to the practitioner. To the natives knowledge of magic means knowledge of spell, and in an analysis of any act of witchcraft it will always be found that the ritual centers round the utterance of the spell. The formula is always the core of the magical performance.

The study of the texts and formulas of primitive magic reveals that there are three typical elements associated with the belief in magical efficiency. There are, first, the phonetic effects, imitations of natural sounds, such as the whistling of the wind, the growling of thunder, the roar of the sea, the voices of various animals. These sounds symbolize certain phenomena and thus are believed to produce them magically. Or else they express certain emo-

tional states associated with the desire which is to be
realized by means of the magic.

The second element, very conspicuous in primitive
spells, is the use of words which invoke, state, or command
the desired aim. Thus the sorcerer will mention all the
symptoms of the disease which he is inflicting, or in the
lethal formula he will describe the end of his victim. In
healing magic the wizard will give word pictures of perfect
health and bodily strength. In economic magic the growing
of plants, the approach of animals, the arrival of fish in
shoals are depicted. Or again the magician uses words and
sentences which express the emotion under the stress of
which he works his magic, and the action which gives expression to this emotion. The sorcerer in tones of fury will
have to repeat such verbs as "I break—I twist—I burn—I
destroy," enumerating with each of them the various parts
of the body and internal organs of his victim. In all this we
see that the spells are built very much on the same pattern
as the rites and the words selected for the same reasons as
the substances of magic.

Thirdly there is an element in almost every spell to which
there is no counterpart in ritual. I mean the mythological
allusions, the references to ancestors and culture heroes
from whom this magic has been received. And that brings
us to perhaps the most important point in the subject, to
the traditional setting of magic.

2. THE TRADITION OF MAGIC   Tradition, which, as we have
several times insisted, reigns supreme in primitive civilization, gathers in great abundance round magical ritual and
cult. In the case of any important magic we invariably find
the story accounting for its existence. Such a story tells
when and where it entered the possession of man, how it
became the property of a local group or of a family or clan.
But such a story is not the story of its origins. Magic never
"originated," it never has been made or invented. All magic
simply "was" from the beginning an essential adjunct of

all such things and processes as vitally interest man and yet elude his normal rational efforts. The spell, the rite, and the thing which they govern are coeval.

Thus, in Central Australia, all magic existed and has been inherited from the *alcheringa* times, when it came about like everything else. In Melanesia all magic comes from a time when humanity lived underground and when magic was a natural knowledge of ancestral man. In higher societies magic is often derived from spirits and demons, but even these, as a rule, originally received and did not invent it. Thus the belief in the primeval natural existence of magic is universal. As its counterpart we find the conviction that only by an absolutely unmodified immaculate transmission does magic retain its efficiency. The slightest alteration from the original pattern would be fatal. There is, then, the idea that between the object and its magic there exists an essential nexus. Magic is the quality of the thing, or rather, of the relation between man and the thing, for though never man-made it is always made for man. In all tradition, in all mythology, magic is always found in the possession of man and through the knowledge of man or man-like being. It implies the performing magician quite as much as the thing to be charmed and the means of charming. It is part of the original endowment of primeval humanity, of the *mura-mura* or *alcheringa* of Australia, of the subterrestrial humanity of Melanesia, of the people of the magical Golden Age all the world over.

Magic is not only human in its embodiment, but also in its subject matter: it refers principally to human activities and states, hunting, gardening, fishing, trading, love-making, disease, and death. It is not directed so much to nature as to man's relation to nature and to the human activities which affect it. Moreover, the effects of magic are usually conceived not as a product of nature influenced by the charm, but as something specially magical, something which nature cannot produce, but only the power of magic. The graver forms of disease, love in its passionate phases, the desire for a ceremonial exchange and other similar mani-

festations in the human organism and mind, are the direct
product of the spell and rite. Magic is thus not derived
from an observation of nature or knowledge of its laws,
it is a primeval possession of man to be known only through
tradition and affirming man's autonomous power of creat-
ing desired ends.

Thus, the force of magic is not a universal force residing
everywhere, flowing where it will or it is willed to. Magic is
the one and only specific power, a force unique of its kind,
residing exclusively in man, let loose only by his magical
art, gushing out with his voice, conveyed by the casting
forth of the rite.

It may be here mentioned that the human body, being
the receptacle of magic and the channel of its flow, must be
submitted to various conditions. Thus the magician has to
keep all sorts of taboos, or else the spell might be injured,
especially as in certain parts of the world, in Melanesia
for instance, the spell resides in the magician's belly, which
is the seat of memory as well as of food. When necessary it
is summoned up to the larynx, which is the seat of intelligence, and thence sent forth by the voice, the main organ
of the human mind. Thus, not only is magic an essentially
human possession, but it is literally and actually enshrined
in man and can be handed on only from man to man, according to very strict rules of magical filiation, initiation,
and instruction. It is thus never conceived as a force of
nature, residing in things, acting independently of man,
to be found out and learned by him, by any of those proceedings by which he gains his ordinary knowledge of nature.

3. MANA AND THE VIRTUE OF MAGIC   The obvious result
of this is that all the theories which lay *mana* and similar
conceptions at the basis of magic are pointing altogether in
the wrong direction. For if the virtue of magic is exclusively
localized in man, can be wielded by him only under very
special conditions and in a traditionally prescribed manner,

it certainly is not a force such as the one described by Dr. Codrington: "This *mana* is not fixed in anything and can be conveyed in almost anything." *Mana* also "acts in all ways for good and evil . . . shows itself in physical force or in any kind of power and excellence which a man possesses." Now it is clear that this force as described by Codrington is almost the exact opposite of the magical virtue as found embodied in the mythology of savages, in their behavior, and in the structure of their magical formulas. For the real virtue of magic, as I know it from Melanesia, is fixed only in the spell and in its rite, and it cannot be "conveyed in" anything, but can be conveyed only by its strictly defined procedure. It never acts "in all ways," but only in ways specified by tradition. It never shows itself in physical force, while its effect upon the powers and excellences of man are strictly limited and defined.

And again, the similar conception found among the North American Indians cannot have anything to do with the specialized concrete virtue of magic. For of the *wakan* of the Dakota we read "all life is *wakan.* So also is everything which exhibits power, whether in action, as the winds and drifting clouds, or in passive endurance, as the boulder by the wayside. . . . It embraces all mystery, all secret power, all divinity." Of the o*renda,* a word taken from the Iroquois, we are told: "This potence is held to be the property of all things . . . the rocks, the waters, the tides, the plants and the trees, the animals and man, the wind and the storms, the clouds and the thunders and the lightnings . . . by the inchoate mentality of man, it is regarded as the efficient cause of all phenomena, all the activities of his environment."

After what has been established about the essence of magical power, it hardly needs emphasizing that there is little in common between the concepts of the *mana* type and the special virtue of magical spell and rite. We have seen that the keynote of all magical belief is the sharp distinction between the traditional force of magic on the one

hand and the other forces and powers with which man and
nature are endowed. The conceptions of the *wakan, orenda,*
and *mana* class which include all sorts of forces and powers,
besides that of magic, are simply an example of an early
generalization of a crude metaphysical concept such as is
found in several other savage words also, extremely important for our knowledge of primitive mentality but, as far as
our present data go, opening only a problem as to the
relation between the early concepts of "force," "the supernatural," and "the virtue of magic." It is impossible to
decide, with the summary information at our disposal, what
is the primary meaning of these compound concepts: that
of physical force and that of supernatural efficiency. In the
American concepts the emphasis seems to be on the former,
in the Oceanic on the latter. What I want to make clear is
that in all the attempts to understand native mentality it
is necessary to study and describe the types of behavior first
and to explain their vocabulary by their customs and their
life. There is no more fallacious guide of knowledge than
language, and in anthropology the "ontological argument"
is specially dangerous.

It was necessary to enter into this problem in detail, for
the theory of *mana* as the essence of primitive magic and
religion has been so brilliantly advocated and so recklessly
handled that it must be realized first that our knowledge of
the *mana,* notably in Melanesia, is somewhat contradictory,
and especially that we have hardly any data at all showing
just how this conception enters into religious or magical
cult and belief.

One thing is certain: magic is not born of an abstract
conception of universal power, subsequently applied to concrete cases. It has undoubtedly arisen independently in a
number of actual situations. Each type of magic, born of
its own situation and of the emotional tension thereof, is
due to the spontaneous flow of ideas and the spontaneous
reaction of man. It is the uniformity of the mental process
in each case which has led to certain universal features of
magic and to the general conceptions which we find at the

basis of man's magical thought and behavior. It will be
necessary to give now an analysis of the situations of magic
and the experiences which they provoke.

4. MAGIC AND EXPERIENCE   So far we have been dealing
mainly with native ideas and with native views of magic.
This has led us to a point where the savage simply affirms
that magic gives man the power over certain things. Now
we must analyze this belief from the point of view of the
sociological observer. Let us realize once more the type of
situation in which we find magic. Man, engaged in a series
of practical activities, comes to a gap; the hunter is disap-
pointed by his quarry, the sailor misses propitious winds,
the canoe builder has to deal with some material of which
he is never certain that it will stand the strain, or the
healthy person suddenly feels his strength failing. What
does man do naturally under such conditions, setting aside
all magic, belief and ritual? Forsaken by his knowledge,
baffled by his past experience and by his technical skill, he
realizes his impotence. Yet his desire grips him only the
more strongly; his anxiety, his fears and hopes, induce a
tension in his organism which drives him to some sort of
activity. Whether he be savage or civilized, whether in possession of magic or entirely ignorant of its existence, passive
inaction, the only thing dictated by reason, is the last thing
in which he can acquiesce. His nervous system and his
whole organism drive him to some substitute activity. Ob-
sessed by the idea of the desired end, he sees it and feels
it. His organism reproduces the acts suggested by the
anticipations of hope, dictated by the emotion of passion
so strongly felt.
   The man under the sway of impotent fury or dominated
by thwarted hate spontaneously clenches his fist and carries
out imaginary thrusts at his enemy, muttering impreca-
tions, casting words of hatred and anger against him. The
lover aching for his unattainable or irresponsive beauty sees
her in his visions, addresses her, and entreats and com-

mands her favors, feeling himself accepted, pressing her to his bosom in his dreams. The anxious fisherman or hunter sees in his imagination the quarry enmeshed in the nets, the animal attained by the spear; he utters their names, describes in words his visions of the magnificent catch, he even breaks out into gestures of mimic representation of what he desires. The man lost at night in the woods or the jungle, beset by superstitious fear, sees around him the haunting demons, addresses them, tries to ward off, to frighten them, or shrinks from them in fear, like an animal which attempts to save itself by feigning death.

These reactions to overwhelming emotion or obsessive desire are natural responses of man to such a situation, based on a universal psycho-physiological mechanism. They engender what could be called extended expressions of emotion in act and in word, the threatening gestures of impotent anger and its maledictions, the spontaneous enactment of the desired end in a practical impasse, the passionate fondling gestures of the lover, and so on. All these spontaneous acts and spontaneous works make man forecast the images of the wished-for results, or express his passion in uncontrollable gestures, or break out into words which give vent to desire and anticipate its end.

And what is the purely intellectual process, the conviction formed during such a free outburst of emotion in words and deeds? First there surges a clear image of the desired end, of the hated person, of the feared danger or ghost. And each image is blended with its specific passion, which drives us to assume an active attitude towards that image. When passion reaches the breaking point at which man loses control over himself, the words which he utters, his blind behavior, allow the pent-up physiological tension to flow over. But over all this outburst presides the image of the end. It supplies the motive-force of the reaction, it apparently organizes and directs words and acts towards a definite purpose. The substitute action in which the passion finds its vent, and which is due to impotence, has subjectively all the value of a real action, to which emotion would, if not impeded, naturally have led.

As the tension spends itself in these words and gestures the obsessing visions fade away, the desired end seems nearer satisfaction, we regain our balance, once more at harmony with life. And we remain with a conviction that the words of malediction and the gestures of fury have traveled towards the hated person and hit their target; that the imploration of love, the visionary embraces, cannot have remained unanswered, that the visionary attainment of success in our pursuit cannot have been without a beneficial influence on the pending issue. In the case of fear, as the emotion which has led us to frenzied behavior gradually subsides, we feel that it is this behavior that has driven away the terrors. In brief, a strong emotional experience, which spends itself in a purely subjective flow of images, words, and acts of behavior, leaves a very deep conviction of its reality, as if of some practical and positive achievement, as if of something done by a power revealed to man. This power, born of mental and physiological obsession, seems to get hold of us from outside, and to primitive man, or to the credulous and untutored mind of all ages, the spontaneous spell, the spontaneous rite, and the spontaneous belief in their efficiency must appear as a direct revelation from some external and no doubt impersonal sources.

When we compare this spontaneous ritual and verbiage of overflowing passion or desire with traditionally fixed magical ritual and with the principles embodied in magical spells and substances, the striking resemblance of the two products shows that they are not independent of each other. Magical ritual, most of the principles of magic, most of its spells and substances, have been revealed to man in those passionate experiences which assail him in the impasses of his instinctive life and of his practical pursuits, in those gaps and breaches left in the ever-imperfect wall of culture which he erects between himself and the besetting temptations and dangers of his destiny. In this I think we have to recognize not only one of the sources but the very fountainhead of magical belief.

To most types of magical ritual, therefore, there corresponds a spontaneous ritual of emotional expression or of a forecast of the desired end. To most features of magical spell, to the commands, invocations, metaphors, there corresponds a natural flow of words, in malediction, in entreaty, in exorcism, and in the descriptions of unfulfilled wishes. To every belief in magical efficiency there can be laid in parallel one of those illusions of subjective experience, transient in the mind of the civilized rationalist, though even there never quite absent, but powerful and convincing to the simple man in every culture, and, above all, to the primitive savage mind.

Thus the foundations of magical belief and practice are not taken from the air, but are due to a number of experiences actually lived through, in which man receives the revelation of his power to attain the desired end. We must now ask: What is the relation between the promises contained in such experience and their fulfillment in real life? Plausible though the fallacious claims of magic might be to primitive man, how is it that they have remained so long unexposed?

The answer to this is that, first, it is a well-known fact that in human memory the testimony of a positive case always overshadows the negative one. One gain easily outweighs several losses. Thus the instances which affirm magic always loom far more conspicuously than those which deny it. But there are other facts which endorse by a real or apparent testimony the claims of magic. We have seen that magical ritual must have originated from a revelation in a real experience. But the man who from such an experience conceived, formulated, and gave to his tribesmen the nucleus of a new magical performance—acting, be it remembered, in perfect good faith—must have been a man of genius. The men who inherited and wielded his magic after him, no doubt always building it out and developing it, while believing that they were simply following up the tradition, must have been always men of great intelligence, energy, and power of enterprise. They would be the men successful in all emergencies. It is an empirical fact that in all savage societies magic and outstanding personality go hand in hand. Thus magic also coincides with personal success, skill, courage, and mental power. No wonder that it is considered a source of success.

This personal renown of the magician and its importance in enhancing the belief about the efficiency of magic are the cause of an interesting phenomenon: what may be called the *current mythology* of magic. Round every big magician there arises a halo made up of stories about his wonderful cures or kills, his catches, his victories, his conquests in love. In every savage society such stories form the backbone of belief in magic, for, supported as they are by the emotional experiences which everyone has had himself, the running chronicle of magical miracles establishes its claims beyond any doubt or cavil. Every eminent practitioner, besides his traditional claim, besides the filiation with his predecessors, makes his personal warrant of wonder-working.

Thus myth is not a dead product of past ages, merely surviving as an idle narrative. It is a living force, constantly producing new phenomena, constantly surrounding magic by new testimonies. Magic moves in the glory of past tradition, but it also creates its atmosphere of ever-nascent myth. As there is the body of legends already fixed, standardized, and constituting the folklore of the tribe, so there is always a stream of narratives in kind to those of the mythological time. Magic is the bridge between the golden age of primeval craft and the wonder-working power of today. Hence the formulas are full of mythical allusions, which, when uttered, unchain the powers of the past and cast them into the present.

With this we see also the role and meaning of mythology in a new light. Myth is not a savage speculation about origins of things born out of philosophic interest. Neither is it the result of the contemplation of nature—a sort of symbolical representation of its laws. It is the historical statement of one of those events which once for all vouch for the truth of a certain form of magic. Sometimes it is the actual record of a magical revelation coming directly from the first man to whom magic was revealed in some dramatic occurrence. More often it bears on its surface that it is merely a statement of how magic came into the possession of a clan or a community or a tribe. In all cases it is a warrant of its truth, a pedigree of its filiation, a charter of its claims to validity. And as we have seen, myth is the natural result of human faith, because every power must give signs of its efficiency, must act and be known to act, if people are to believe in its virtue. Every belief engenders its mythology, for there is no faith without miracles, and the main myth recounts simply the primeval miracle of the magic.

Myth, it may be added at once, can attach itself not only to magic but to any form of social power or social claim. It is used always to account for extraordinary privileges or duties, for great social inequalities, for severe burdens of rank, whether this be very high or very low. Also the beliefs and powers of religion are traced to their sources by mythological accounts. Religious myth, however, is rather an explicit dogma, the belief in the nether world, in creation, in the nature of divinities, spun out into a story. Sociological myth, on the other hand, especially in primitive cultures, is usually blended with legends about the sources of magical power. It can be said without exaggeration that the most typical, most highly developed, mythology in primitive societies is that of magic, and the function of myth is not to explain but to vouch for, not to satisfy curiosity but to give confidence in power, not to spin out yarns but to establish the flowing freely from present-day occurrences, frequently similar validity of belief. The deep connection between myth and cult, the pragmatic function of myth in enforcing belief, has been so persistently overlooked in favor of the etiological or explanatory theory of myth that it was necessary to dwell on this point.

5. MAGIC AND SCIENCE We have had to make a digression on mythology since we found that myth is engendered by the real or imaginary success of witchcraft. But what about its failures? With all the strength which magic draws from the spontaneous belief and spontaneous ritual of intense desire or thwarted emotion, with all the force given it by the personal prestige, the social power and success common in the magician and practitioner—still there are failures and breakdowns, and we should vastly underrate the savage's intelligence, logic, and grasp of experience if we assumed that he is not aware of it and that he fails to account for it.

First of all, magic is surrounded by strict conditions: exact remembrance of a spell, unimpeachable performance of the rite, unswerving adhesion to the taboos and observances which shackle the magician. If any one of these is neglected, failure of magic follows. And then, even if magic be done in the most perfect manner, its effects can be equally well undone: for against every magic there can be also counter-magic. If magic, as we have shown, is begotten by the union of man's steadfast desire with the wayward whim of chance, then every desire, positive or negative, may—nay, must—have its magic. Now in all his social and worldly ambitions, in all his strivings to catch good fortune and trap propitious luck, man moves in an atmosphere of rivalry, of envy, and of spite. For luck, possessions, even health, are matters of degree and of comparison, and if your neighbor owns more cattle, more wives, more health, and more power than yourself, you feel dwarfed in all you own and all you are. And such is human nature that a man's desire is as much satisfied by the thwarting of others as by the advancement of himself. To this sociological play of desire and counter-desire, of ambition and spite, of success and envy, there corresponds the play of magic and counter-magic, or of magic white and black.

In Melanesia, where I have studied this problem at firsthand, there is not one single magical act which is not firmly believed to possess a counter-act which, when stronger, can completely annihilate its effects. In certain types of magic, as for instance, that of health and disease, the formulas actually go in couples. A sorcerer who learns a performance by which to cause a definite disease will at the same time learn the formula and the rite which can annul completely the effects of his evil magic. In love, again, not only does there exist a belief that, when two formulas are performed to win the same heart, the stronger will override the weaker one, but there are spells uttered directly to alienate the affections of the sweetheart or wife of another. Whether this duality of magic is as consistently carried out all the world over as in the Trobriands it is difficult to say, but that the twin forces of white and black, of positive and negative, exist everywhere is beyond doubt. Thus the failures of magic can always be accounted for by the slip of memory, by slovenliness in performance or in observance of a taboo, and, last not least, by the fact that someone else has performed some counter-magic.

We are now in a position to state more fully the relation between magic and science already outlined above. Magic is akin to science in that it always has a definite aim intimately associated with human instincts, needs, and pursuits. The magic art is directed towards the attainment of practical aims. Like the other arts and crafts, it is also governed by a theory, by a system of principles which dictate the manner in which the act has to be performed in order to be effective. In analyzing magical spells, rites, and substances we have found that there are a number of general principles which govern them. Both science and magic develop a special technique. In magic, as in the other arts, man can undo what he has done or mend the damage which he has wrought. In fact, in magic, the quantitive equivalents of black and white seem to be much more exact and the effects of witchcraft much more completely eradicated by counter-witchcraft than is possible in any practical art or craft. Thus both magic and science show certain similarities, and, with Sir James Frazer, we can appropriately call magic a pseudo-science.

And the spurious character of this pseudo-science is not hard to detect. Science, even as represented by the primitive knowledge of savage man, is based on the normal universal experience of everyday life, experience won in man's struggle with nature for his subsistence and safety, founded on observation, fixed by reason. Magic is based on specific experience of emotional states in which man observes not nature but himself, in which the truth is revealed not by reason but by the play of emotions upon the human organism. Science is founded on the conviction that experience, effort, and reason are valid; magic on the belief that hope cannot fail nor desire deceive. The theories of knowledge are dictated by logic, those of magic by the association of ideas under the influence of desire. As a matter of empirical fact the body of rational knowledge and the body of magical lore are incorporated each in a different tradition, in a different social setting and in a different type of activity, and all these differences are clearly recognized by the savages. The one constitutes the domain of the profane; the other, hedged round by observances, mysteries, and taboos, makes up half of the domain of the sacred.

6. MAGIC AND RELIGION   Both magic and religion arise and function in situations of emotional stress: crises of life, lacunae in important pursuits, death and initiation into tribal mysteries, unhappy love and unsatisfied hate. Both magic and religion open up escapes from such situations and such impasses as offer no empirical way out except by ritual and belief into the domain of the supernatural. This domain embraces, in religion, beliefs in ghosts, spirits, the primitive forebodings of providence, the guardians of tribal mysteries; in magic, the primeval force and virtue of magic. Both magic and religion are based strictly on mythological tradition, and they also both exist in the atmosphere of the miraculous, in a constant revelation of their wonder-

working power. They both are surrounded by taboos and
observances which mark off their acts from those of the
profane world.

Now what distinguishes magic from religion? We have
taken for our starting-point a most definite and tangible
distinction: we have defined, within the domain of the
sacred, magic as a practical art consisting of acts which are
only means to a definite end expected to follow later on;
religion as a body of self-contained acts being themselves
the fulfillment of their purpose. We can now follow up
this difference into its deeper layers. The practical art of
magic has its limited, circumscribed technique: spell, rite,
and the condition of the performer form always its trite
trinity. Religion, with its complex aspects and purposes,
has no such simple technique, and its unity can be seen
neither in the form of its acts nor even in the uniformity
of its subject matter, but rather in the function which it
fulfills and in the value of its belief and ritual. Again, the
belief in magic, corresponding to its plain practical nature,
is extremely simple. It is always the affirmation of man's
power to cause certain definite effects by a definite spell
and rite. In religion, on the other hand, we have a whole
supernatural world of faith: the pantheon of spirits and
demons, the benevolent powers of totem, guardian spirit,
tribal all-father, the vision of the future life, create a second
supernatural reality for primitive man. The mythology of
religion is also more varied and complex as well as more
creative. It usually centers round the various tenets of belief, and it develops them into cosmogonies, tales of culture
heroes, accounts of the doings of gods and demigods. In
magic, important as it is, mythology is an ever-recurrent
boasting about man's primeval achievements.

Magic, the specific art for specific ends, has in every one
of its forms come once into the possession of man, and it
had to be handed over in direct filiation from generation to
generation. Hence it remains from the earliest times in the
hands of specialists, and the first profession of mankind is
that of a wizard or witch. Religion, on the other hand, in

primitive conditions is an affair of all, in which everyone
takes an active and equivalent part. Every member of the
tribe has to go through initiation, and then himself initiates
others. Everyone wails, mourns, digs the grave and com-
memorates, and in due time everyone has his turn in being
mourned and commemorated. Spirits are for all, and everyone becomes a spirit. The only specialization in religion—
that is, early spiritualistic mediumism—is not a profession
but a personal gift. One more difference between magic and
religion is the play of black and white in witchcraft, while
religion in its primitive stages has but little of the contrast
between good and evil, between the beneficent and malevolent powers. This is due also to the practical character
of magic, which aims at direct quantitative results, while
early religion, though essentially moral, has to deal with
fateful, irremediable happenings and supernatural forces
and beings, so that the undoing of things done by man
does not enter into it. The maxim that fear first made gods
in the universe is certainly not true in the light of anthropology.

In order to grasp the difference between religion and
magic and to gain a clear vision of the three-cornered constellation of magic, religion, and science, let us briefly
realize the cultural function of each. The function of
primitive knowledge and its value have been assessed already and indeed are not difficult to grasp. By acquainting
man with his surroundings, by allowing him to use the
forces of nature, science, primitive knowledge, bestows on
man an immense biological advantage, setting him far
above all the rest of creation. The function of religion and
its value we have learned to understand in the survey of
savage creeds and cults given above. We have shown there
that religious faith establishes, fixes, and enhances all valuable mental attitudes, such as reverence for tradition, harmony with environment, courage and confidence in the
struggle with difficulties and at the prospect of death. This
belief, embodied and maintained by cult and ceremonial,

has an immense biological value, and so reveals to primitive man truth in the wider, pragmatic sense of the word.

What is the cultural function of magic? We have seen that all the instincts and emotions, all practical activities, lead man into impasses where gaps in his knowledge and the limitations of his early power of observation and reason betray him at a crucial moment. Human organism reacts to this in spontaneous outbursts, in which rudimentary modes of behavior and rudimentary beliefs in their efficiency are engendered. Magic fixes upon these beliefs and rudimentary rites and standardizes them into permanent traditional forms. Thus magic supplies primitive man with a number of ready-made ritual acts and beliefs, with a definite mental and practical technique which serves to bridge over the dangerous gaps in every important pursuit or critical situation. It enables man to carry out with confidence his important tasks, to maintain his poise and his mental integrity in fits of anger, in the throes of hate, of unrequited love, of despair and anxiety. The function of magic is to ritualize man's optimism, to enhance his faith in the victory of hope over fear. Magic expresses the greater value for man of confidence over doubt, of steadfastness over vacillation, of optimism over pessimism.

Looking from far and above, from our high places of safety in developed civilization, it is easy to see all the crudity and irrelevance of magic. But without its power and guidance early man could not have mastered his practical difficulties as he has done, nor could man have advanced to the higher stages of culture. Hence the universal occurrence of magic in primitive societies and its enormous sway. Hence do we find magic an invariable adjunct of all important activities. I think we must see in it the embodiment of the sublime folly of hope, which has yet been the best school of man's character.[1]

[1] *Bibliographical Note.* The most important works on Primitive Religion, Magic and Knowledge, referred to in the text, directly or implicitly, are: E. B. Tylor, *Primitive Culture,* 4th ed., 2 vols., 1903; J. F. McLennan, *Studies in*

Ancient History, 1886; W. Robertson Smith, Lectures on the Religion of the Semites, 1889; A. Lang, The Making of Religion, 1889, and Magic and Religion, 1901. These, though out of date as regards material and some of their conclusions, are still inspiring and deserve study. Entirely fresh and representing the most modern points of view are the classical works of J. G. Frazer, The Golden Bough, 3rd ed., in 12 vols., 1911–14 (also abridged edition, 1 vol.) Totemism and Exogamy, 4 vols., 1910; Folk-Lore in the Old Testament, 3 vols., 1919; The Belief in Immortality and the Worship of the Dead, so far 3 vols., 1913–24. With Frazer's works should be read the two excellent contributions of E. Crawley, The Mystic Rose, 1902 (out of print, new edition forthcoming), and The Tree of Life, 1905. Also on the subject of the history of morals, the two extremely important works: E. Westermarck, The Origin and Development of the Moral Ideas, 2 vols., 1905, and L. T. Hobhouse, Morals in Evolution, 2nd ed., 1915. Further: D. G. Brinton, Religions of Primitive Peoples, 1899; K. Th. Preuss, Der Ursprung der Religion und Kunst, 1904 (in "Globus," serially); R. R. Marett, The Threshold of Religion, 1909; H. Hubert et M. Mauss, Mélanges d'histoire des religions, 1909; A. van Gennep, Les Rites de passage, 1909; J. Harrison, Themis 1910–12; I. King, The Development of Religion, 1910; W. Schmidt, Der Ursprung der Gottesidee, 1912; E. Durkheim, Les Formes élementaires de la Vie religieuse, 1912 (also English translation); P. Ehrenreich, Die Allgemeine Mythologie, 1910; R. H. Lowie, Primitive Religion, 1925. An encyclopedic survey of facts and opinions will be found in Wilh. Wundt's voluminous Volkerpsychologie, 1904 ff.; J. Hastings' Encyclopedia of Religion and Ethics is excellent and indispensable to the serious student. Primitive Knowledge in particular is discussed by Lévy-Bruhl in Les fonctions mentales dans les sociétés inférieures, 1910; F. Boas, The Mind of Primitive Man, 1910; R. Thurnwald, Psychologie des Primitiven Menschen, in the Handbuch der vergl. Psychol., edited by G. Kafka, 1922; A. A. Goldenwasser, Early Civilization, 1923. Cf. also R. H. Lowie, Primitive Society, 1920; and A. L. Kroeber, Anthropology, 1923. For fuller information upon the natives of Melanesia, who loom largely in the foregoing descriptions, cf. R. H. Codrington, The Melanesians, 1891; C. G. Seligman, The Melanesians of British New Guinea, 1910; R. Thurnwald, Forschungen auf den Solominseln und Bismarckarchipel, 2 vols., 1912, and Die Gemeinde der Bánaro, 1921; B. Malinowski, The

Natives of Mailu, 1915 (in Trans. of the R. Soc. of S. Australia, vol. xxxix); *Baloma,* article in the Journ. of the R. Anthrop. Institute, 1916; *Argonauts of the Western Pacific,* 1922; and three articles in *Psyche,* III., 2; IV., 4; V., 3, 1923–5.

www.ingramcontent.com/pod-product-compliance
Lightning Source LLC
Chambersburg PA
CBHW050550280326
41933CB00011B/1789